Live in a Home that

PAYS YOU BACK

ANNA DESIMONE

Technical Review:

Jim Nostedt, P. Eng.
Winnipeg, Manitoba

Live in a Home that Pays You Back

FriesenPress

Suite 300 - 990 Fort St
Victoria, BC, V8V 3K2
Canada

www.friesenpress.com

First Edition — 2021

ISBN
978-1-03-912349-6 (Hardcover)
978-1-03-912348-9 (Paperback)
978-1-03-912350-2 (eBook)

1. BUSINESS & ECONOMICS, REAL ESTATE

Distributed to the trade by The Ingram Book Company

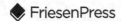

Acknowledgments

Special thanks to Jim Nostedt, P. Eng. from SEEFAR Building Analytics Inc. in Winnipeg, Manitoba, for his valuable technical review services. Thanks to the absolute best copy editor, Doris Castagno. Thanks to Joanna Breen, the production team at FriesenPress, the Jenkins Group, and Jane Reilly at Smith Publicity.

Special thanks to the environmental visionaries and industry leaders who shared their time and expertise: Sam Rashkin, TruHome Facts; Joe Emerson, Zero Energy Project; Robert J. Pierson, ECOHome; Wayne Cole, SEEFAR Building Analytics Inc.; Brett Cass, Canadian Home Builders Association; Donna Peak, Log &Timber Home Living Magazine; Dan Mitchell, Eagle CDI Builders; and Andrew Morrison, DMI AccuSystems.

Cover design:	Yvonne Fetig Roehler, Jenkins Group, Inc.
Cover photo:	Shutterstock
Infographics:	Shutterstock
Author photo:	NYC Portraits

Contents

Chapter 10

Rebates and Incentives 163

CHAPTER 1

Why Invest in an Energy-efficient Home?

WHAT IS THE PAYBACK? When we think about payback, we tend to think in financial terms, such as the break-even point, or return on investment. These are meaningful questions when you're exploring mortgage options. However, with an energy-efficient home, payback is quantified a number of different ways.

Today's homebuyers want sustainability—not just for home construction features, but to maintain long-term affordability as well. The best part about investing in "the home of the future" is that it will sustain your plan for the future.

With an energy-efficient home, your "true cost of homeownership" will be lower. Monthly utility bills are lower, construction materials are more durable, and appliances require fewer repairs and maintenance. Expanded mortgage programs will boost your buying power, and you will have access to many rebates and financial incentives. Energy-efficient homes increase in value at a faster rate than traditional homes, adding more dollars to your retirement nest egg.

In this chapter we take a look at five types of payback, and begin with a type of payback that is immeasurable—***your family's health.***

1. Your Home Will Be Healthier.

Scientific advancements in ventilation systems are now able to capture far greater levels of bacteria, allergens, and airborne pollutants. Your family can benefit from a continuous supply of fresh, filtered air. Energy-efficient homes are constructed with non-toxic materials and include built-in protections from mold and other environmental contaminants.

Research completed by the Joint Center for Housing Studies at Harvard University found that consumers are increasingly worried about the link between health and everyday environmental exposures. In its study, *Healthy Home Remodeling: Consumer Trends and Contractor Preparedness,*[1] the Joint Center found that "indoor air quality" ranked as the leading source of concern. Other pressing concerns included moisture, mold, water quality, and harmful chemicals such as radon.

Data from the study showed that 30% of households expressed concerns about some aspect of their home negatively impacting or posing a risk to their health. Among homeowners surveyed, the most common reason cited for exploring remediation steps was that a household member had developed physical symptoms.[2]

> **As of 2019, web searches on Google for the term "non-toxic" marginally outpaced even those for the term "energy efficient."**
>
> —Harvard University Joint Center for Housing Studies

According to a report completed by the U.S. Department of Energy (DOE), *Home Rx: The Health Benefits of Home Performance,*[3] energy-efficient enhancements can change the physical environment of homes by stabilizing temperatures, enhancing indoor air quality, and improving environmental conditions.

The DOE report analyzed data from 300 technical articles and a total of 44 studies conducted in the United States, Canada, and other countries around the world. The report identified that energy-efficient enhancements typically completed by builders and home improvement contractors have proven to directly impact health.

The DOE study examined variables from homes with occupants who had pre-existing health conditions, as well as adults and children with asthma. Results showed improvements in overall physical and mental health, respiratory health, and reduced injuries for homes that were constructed or renovated in accordance with "green building" standards.[4]

A report completed by the International Energy Agency (IEA), *Capturing the Multiple Benefits of Energy Efficiency,*[5] examined health outcomes resulting from energy-efficient measures.

A number of efficiency measures were studied, including insulation, air sealing, improved heating systems, improved cooking systems, and ventilation. Each measure was analyzed for its primary housing effect, secondary housing effect, and expected health outcomes.

Results from every type of measure indicated "reduced symptoms of respiratory disease." Examples of other health outcomes were telling. For example, in addition to a reduced risk of respiratory disease, the "ventilation" efficiency measure also indicated a reduced risk of cancer, cardiovascular disease, arthritis, and depression.[6]

2. Your Home Will Be More Comfortable.

Efficient lighting systems improve light distribution, reduce eyestrain, and offer a more calming atmosphere. High-performance heating and cooling systems deliver more consistent heating and cooling temperatures throughout every room in the house. Newer systems are quieter and available with programmable thermostats so that you can schedule temperature changes that fit your daily routine.

Maximum thermal insulation, along with high-performance windows, keep your home warmer in the winter and cooler in the summer. Thermal insulation and weatherization techniques keep those surprise drafts away when you're trying to relax. Sometimes comfort is simply a peace of mind, as expressed by the Yale Center for Environmental Communication at Yale University based on a study by the Urban Green Council.[7]

> **Even during a winter blackout, you can expect a high-efficiency home to stay warm for several days.**
>
> —Yale Climate Connections

3. Your Home Will Use Less Energy.

A home's energy efficiency is based on a whole-house assessment. Known as an "energy score," the efficiency rating of a home is based on measurable performance factors of individual appliances or operating systems. As upgrades or other efficiencies are integrated into the home, energy requirements will continue to drop.

According to Energy Star, Energy Star certified homes are at least 15% more energy efficient than standard homes; however, due to additional energy-saving features, homes are typically 20–30% more efficient.[8]

Energy consumption in residential homes has continued to increase even though there are many new technologies to conserve energy. The size of homes in the U.S. has increased 41 percent since the 1970s, while the average number of occupants has decreased 15 percent during the same period.[9]

Wasteful energy consumption includes heating and cooling of unoccupied homes and rooms, and accounts for at least 45% of total energy use in the residential sector, as reported in the *2020 Annual Energy Outlook* prepared by the U.S. Energy Information Administration (EIA).[10]

The Consumer Technology Association estimates the average household owns 24 home electronics products. Typically, a home includes at least three televisions, a cable box, a game console, a DVR, three home audio devices, and lots of chargers.[11]

> **In 2019, electricity for miscellaneous household devices consumed more electricity than the core requirements for heating, water-heating, cooling, and refrigeration.[12]**
>
> —Center for Sustainable Systems, University of Michigan

Residential energy use in the United States in 2019 averaged 33.91% for space heating and 11.04% for cooling, according to the Center for Sustainable Systems at the University of Michigan.[13]

Natural Resources Canada reports that 61.6% of residential energy consumption in Canadian households is used for space heating, and 1.9% for cooling.[14]

4. You Will Reduce Greenhouse Gas Emissions.

Most primary sources of energy are non-sustainable. About 80% of energy sources in North America come from "fossil fuels." Coal, crude oil, and natural gas are considered fossil fuels because they were formed from the fossilized, buried remains of plants and animals that lived millions of years ago.

Because of their origins, fossil fuels have a high carbon content. Fossil fuels are now being replaced with "renewable" sources, also referred to as "clean energy." Renewable energy comes from Earth's natural sources that are constantly being replenished.[15]

The "greenhouse effect" is a natural phenomenon that insulates Earth from the cold of space. Greenhouse gas (GHG) emissions are comprised of atmospheric GHGs, and emissions that are caused by humans, known as "anthropogenic" emissions. Greenhouse gas emissions consist of carbon dioxide (CO_2), methane (CH_4), and nitrous oxide (N_2O).

Human-caused emissions are modifying Earth's energy balance between incoming solar radiation and the heat released back into space, which amplifies the greenhouse effect and results in climate change.[16]

According to the U.S. Environmental Protection Agency (EPA), the largest source of human-caused greenhouse gas emissions is from burning fossil fuels for electricity, heat, and transportation.[17]

> **The global warming potential (GWP) of GHG emissions is calculated as carbon dioxide equivalents (CO_2e) as a single unit for measurement. This measurement unit is known as a carbon footprint.[18]**
>
> —Center for Sustainable Systems, University of Michigan

The EPA defines a carbon footprint as: "The total amount of greenhouse gases that are emitted into the atmosphere each year by a person, family, building, organization, or company."

The EPA's *Household Carbon Footprint Calculator* establishes a household's carbon footprint based on geographic location, automobile miles driven, type of heating fuel, electricity use, and recycling or composting activity.[19]

According to the Center for Sustainable Systems at the University of Michigan, as of September 2020 the typical U.S. household had a carbon footprint of 48 metric tons of carbon dioxide (CO_2), and an "individual carbon footprint" of 20.4 metric tons per year.[20]

The "Paris Agreement" is a landmark environmental accord that was adopted in 2015 by nearly every nation in the world. The Agreement aims to limit the global temperature increase in this century to 2 degrees Celsius above pre-industrial levels, and to pursue efforts to limit the temperature rise to 1.5 degrees Celsius.[21]

On November 19, 2020, the House of Commons of Canada passed a bill to achieve "net-zero" greenhouse gas emissions by the year 2050. The purpose of the Act is to set national targets for the reduction of greenhouse gas emissions based on the best scientific information available and to promote transparency.[22] As of November 2020, net-zero targets had been pledged by ten countries around the world.[23]

Homeowners today have a number of options to offset grid-connected utilities with a renewable source of energy. More than 2 million Americans have installed solar energy systems in their homes.[24] The United States generates the most geothermal electricity in the world.[25]

In Canada, 67% of electricity comes from renewable sources, and 82% from non-GHG emitting sources.[26] Canada is the world's third-largest producer of hydroelectricity,[27] and nearly 3.5 million Canadian homeowners are powering their homes with wind turbines.[28]

5. You Will Have Greater Financial Rewards.

According to the U.S. Department of Energy, the typical household can save 25% on utility bills with efficiency measures, which amounts to over $2,200 annually.[29]

Across the United States and Canada, there are more than 2,000 incentives available to residential homeowners to help cover the cost of efficient appliances and energy-efficiency measures. Many utility companies offer free energy assessments and discounts to complete recommended measures.

Cash rebates are available from numerous appliance manufacturers. Incentives are available to support all types of efficiency improvements, including measures such as air-sealing and weatherization.

Should you choose to install a renewable energy system such as solar photovoltaic (PV) panels, you may be eligible for federal tax credits, as well as state and local tax credits or deductions. Many cities and towns have issued property tax waivers so that you are not taxed for the increase in value after installing a renewable energy system.

When you apply for a mortgage, the projected savings in utility costs will be added to your income if you apply for an "energy-efficient mortgage" program, which eases loan qualification. If you plan to upgrade your home with additional energy features in the future, there are many zero-interest energy improvement loans and grants from housing partnership agencies.

Your long-term investment will be more secure. A study completed by the North Carolina Building Performance Association revealed that homes with green certification programs such as Energy Star sold for 9.5% more than non-certified homes.[30]

SEEFAR Building Analytics Inc., based in Winnipeg, Manitoba, has developed a software tool that monetizes building sustainability. The SEEFAR valuation tool incorporates a 60-year life-cycle analysis, which is used in home appraisals to support energy features, determine long-term investment value, and supports access to mortgage financing. Sustainable homes are constructed with more long-lasting materials. Due to fewer replacements of materials and appliances, homeowners are also reducing their greenhouse gas emissions.[31]

> Making a home more durable reduces carbon. Making a home more energy efficient reduces cost.
>
> —Wayne Cole, SEEFAR Building Analytics Inc.

CHAPTER 2

Whole House Efficiency Blueprint

THINK LIKE A BUILDING CONTRACTOR. This chapter examines five main parts of the house—the building envelope; thermal enclosure; heating, cooling, and ventilation; lighting and appliances; and water management. You'll have a close look at how some high-performance systems work and discover some new trends along the way.

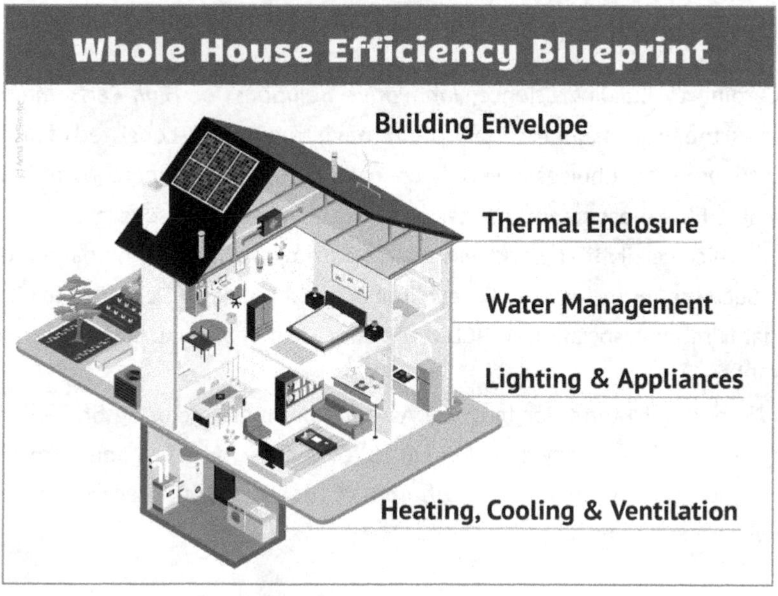

BLUEPRINT #1

Building Envelope

The building envelope represents the outer layer of a home. Think of your home as a six-sided box, encompassing the four walls, roof, and foundation level. Sometimes the building envelope is called a "building enclosure."

The building envelope serves as a physical separator between the conditioned and unconditioned environment. It provides resistance to air, water, heat, light, and noise. The builder's objective is to make your home airtight and well insulated so that the energy that comes into the home stays within the envelope.

The building envelope protects exterior materials from deteriorating in bad weather. Homes are designed so that rain and melting snow are directed away from the roof, walls, and foundation. "Drainage planes," which are made from moisture-resistant material, are installed in continuous overlapping layers. The area around the home is graded so that water flows away from the foundation and is directed to underground drains. "Flashing" is a second layer of protection that is installed at roof-to-wall intersections and around windows and doors.

Exterior Siding

According to Building Science, *Innovative Solutions for High-Performance Homes,* the three major exterior options have traditionally consisted of brick, stucco, or wood. Choices generally conform to the local climate. Wood has remained the most common exterior siding, and there are several organizations which certify that wood was sourced from a sustainably managed forest. Such groups include the Forest Stewardship Council (FSC), Western Red Cedar Lumber Association (WRCLA) and the Cedar Shake and Shingle Bureau (CSSB).[32]

According to the Brick Industry Association, manufacturing brick today requires 70% less energy than it did in 1970. Because brick is made from clay and sand, it is non-toxic, fireproof, impact resistant, 100% recyclable, and provides thermal mass.

Brick and stone can be applied as a veneer rather than structural material. "Stucco" is a versatile material that can be directly applied to solid masonry, concrete, or "insulated concrete forms" known as ICFs.[33]

"Fiber cement" is made from a mixture of sand, wood fibers, cement, and water. Products are fire resistant, low maintenance, long lasting, and can mimic wood siding, clapboard, shingle, and board and batten. Fiber cement siding was first engineered by James Hardie Building Products, which manufacture *Hardie Plank, Hardie Shingle, Artisan*, and others. The Hardie companies are committed to a *Zero Harm Initiative*.[34]

KWP is an ecologically conscious manufacturer of engineered wood products. Siding and trim board are available in a variety of colors, styles, and textures, including a product with the look of authentic cedar shakes. KWP's *Eco-Side* collection uses 100% recycled post-industrial content.

Innovations in sustainable siding materials include architectural panels under the brand *Allura*, manufactured by Plycem. Other products such as *SmartSide* and *Progressive Foam* combine exterior siding with insulation.

"Steel siding" is a coated, long-lasting option available in many colors and textures. Other options include *Satinwood* and *Kynar*, which have special coatings similar to Teflon.

"Acetylated wood products" offer improved thermal insulation, longer life span, and better dimensional stability. Products resist decay and are considered an alternative to using toxic pressure-treated wood. "Structured Insulated Panels," known as SIPs, are airtight, insulated building systems that provide thermal resistance.

"Mass timber" is an alternative to steel or concrete and offers a very high strength-to-weight ratio. Layering methods include cross-laminated timber and glue-laminated timber. "Rammed Earth" is made from soil that is bound, placed in layers, and pressurized to create a hard surface for floors and walls. The finished look is very smooth and resembles sedimentary rock.

"Bamboo" is one of the world's fastest growing plants and is considered an excellent alternative to wood. Bamboo is often used for decks, floors, and cabinetry. "Straw bales" are made from agricultural industry vegetation waste. When straw bales are used for exterior walls, the walls are thicker and keep the home well-insulated.

Roofs

According to Green Builder, wood is the only renewable product available; products are also available from reclaimed wood sources. Wood is popular in areas where wood is harvested, such as the Pacific Northwest, Midwest, New England, and most Canadian provinces. There are certain geographical areas where building codes restrict wood use due to dry weather conditions.[35]

Asphalt shingles remain the popular choice, and in certain geographic regions, tiles made from clay, ceramic, or concrete are widely used. The latest sustainable trend is "metal roofs," which are considered highly efficient and low maintenance. Types of metal used in roofing include steel, copper, aluminum, and zinc. Products are available in a wide assortment of colors and architectural styles, including some that resemble shingles or slate. According to the U.S. Green Building Council, metal roofing typically contains a minimum of 25% recycled materials.[36]

Solar Roof Shingles

Scientific advancements in solar energy products continue to deliver new and exciting products to the home building industry. Solar shingles resemble conventional roofing materials while also producing electricity. Manufacturers include Tesla, CertainTeed, SolarCity, and RGS Energy.

Green Roofs

A green roof is a layer of vegetation that is planted over a waterproofing system installed on top of a flat or slightly sloped roof. Green roofs, also known as vegetative or eco-roofs, can support a diverse range of plants, including small trees. Green roofs absorb carbon dioxide, help insulate the building, and can increase the life expectancy of the roofing system.[37]

"Thatched" roofs, which are made from hay, straw, reed, sedge, and other dry vegetation, have been used for centuries and are most widely seen in the English countryside and Europe. Thatching works well in tropical climates and is used by builders in developing countries. The densely packed materials trap air, which insulates the home. Thatch is now becoming a popular trend in high-end, custom-built homes.

BLUEPRINT #2

Thermal Enclosure

There are four imperatives required to optimize the thermal enclosure of a home: maximum insulation, efficient air sealing, strong moisture barriers, and high-performance windows and doors.

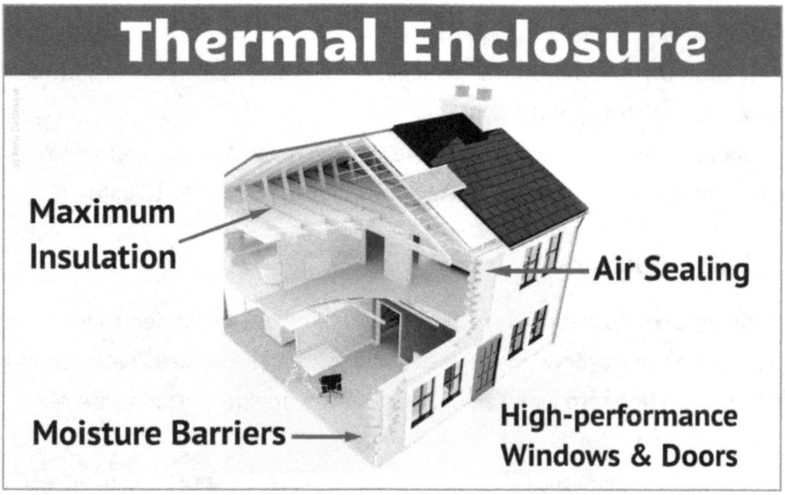

Insulation

R-value means "resistance to heat flow." The higher the R-value, the more resistance is being provided by the insulation. R-value requirements vary based on geographical area and the part of the home that is being insulated. Typical recommendations for exterior walls range from R-13 to R-23, and the range is R-30 to R-49 for an attic and the space above ceilings.

"Thermal bridging" is a term that is used to describe targeted insulation applied to areas surrounding the support beams and studs. When structural bridging areas between floors and walls remain uninsulated, they will lower the R-value in that part of the house.

According to Home Innovation Research Labs, as of 2019 fiberglass remained the number one insulation for home builders.[38] Fiberglass insulation is available in a wide number of forms—long rolls, blankets (or batts), concrete blocks, rigid foam, and boards. Some insulation products are delivered through spraying devices, such as "loose-fill" and "foam."

Eco-friendly Insulation

Many different types of insulation are considered sustainable, however, there are some eco-friendly products worth mentioning.

"Denim cotton" is blue-colored insulation made from recycled blue jeans and denim cotton. Unlike fiberglass, handling the insulation does not irritate skin.

"Cellulose" insulation products are made from 85% recycled content, primarily newsprint. Other materials used in cellulose insulation include cardboard, cotton, straw, and sawdust.

"Sheep's wool" is considered one of the most natural and renewable sources of insulation, and products are available with an R-19 value.

Insulation Cautions

Certain types of insulation have been found to be unsafe. Older homes sometimes contain hazardous insulation, some of which require "safe removal" procedures. There are licensed professionals who specialize in safe removal of asbestos and other hazardous materials.

"Asbestos insulation" is highly toxic when fibers become airborne. Asbestos has not been produced in the United States since 1978.

"Vermiculite" was a popular form of insulation for many years. Prior to 1990, however, about 70% of vermiculite was contaminated with asbestos due to shared manufacturing facilities.

"Urea Formaldehyde Foam Insulation (UFFI)" was used in homes during the 1970s and early 1980s. The product has been discredited for its toxic emissions and is used only for industrial applications or in commercial buildings.

"Fiberglass" is made from extremely fine glass fibers and can be hazardous when improperly handled. In addition to skin irritations, fibers can be absorbed into airborne dust and irritate the eyes, nose, and throat.

"Mineral wool," which is often used for insulation in the form of "rock wool," requires the same handling precautions as fiberglass.

The following chart provides a brief description of various types of home insulation, based on information from the U.S. Department of Energy.[39]

Types of Insulation	
Cellulose	Made from 85% recycled paper products, primarily newsprint. Generally loose-fill in open attic areas, and dense-packed in building cavities and between walls.
Cementitious Foam	Cement-based foam, known as Krete or Airkrete. Non-toxic, nonflammable, and made from minerals extracted from seawater.
Cotton & Denim Cotton	Natural fiber consisting of 85% recycled cotton and 15% plastic fibers. Available in batts; includes flame-retardant and insect-repellent treatments.
Fiberglass	Made from fiber-reinforced plastic materials embedded with microscopic glass filaments. Available as blown insulation, in various sizes of batts and rolls with a variety of facings.
Insulation Facings	Fastened to insulation materials during the manufacturing process. Some types act as a vapor barrier, a radiant barrier, or a barrier to air.
Phenolic Foam	Currently available only as foamed-in-place insulation. May be found in older homes as rigid board.
Polyiso	Scientific name is polyisocyanurate, and available as liquid and sprayed foam and rigid foam board. Can be laminated for use in structural insulated panels (SIPs).
Polystyrene	Colorless, transparent thermoplastic that is commonly used to make foam board, beadboard, or concrete block insulation. Molded expanded polystyrene is used for foam insulation.
Polyurethane	Foam insulation available in liquid sprayed foam or rigid foam board. Can also be made into laminated panels with a variety of facings.
Rock Wool	Rock wool is fibrous material that is made by spinning mineral rock and slag. Used for structural and pipe insulation and soundproofing.
Sheep's Wool	Treated to resist pests, fire, and mold. Can hold large quantities of water. Batts available up to R-19 value.
Straw	Straw is fused into boards without adhesives and has effective sound-absorbing properties.

Air Sealing

The uninvited guest that leaks into the house starts out as air—and later becomes moisture. Air likes to move by the easiest path available. Air naturally moves from high-pressure areas to low-pressure areas through a hole or crack in the house.

The integrity of the exterior walls is the first line of defense for preventing damage to building materials and impairing indoor air quality. Air sealing controls the movement of air and guards the home against heat loss.

"Uncontrolled moisture" can enter the home through window and door openings, seams, footings, roofs, or other openings. An exterior weather barrier is installed to prevent moisture from entering construction cavities.

Water can also enter construction cavities through a process called "moisture migration," which can cause mold in any type of climate. Air sealing steps can reduce condensation, leaks, and drafts. Techniques include the application of caulk, foams, specialty tapes, and adhesives.

> **A typical home contains a half-mile of cracks and gaps behind walls and around windows and doors, along with dozens of holes for pipes, vents, ducts, lighting, and wiring.[40]**
>
> —Energy Star

Moisture Barriers

"Foundation moisture control" is a strategy to ensure potential moisture problems do not occur in the basement, crawlspace, or slab-on-grade foundation. Such areas need to be insulated to properly control moisture.

"Vapor barriers" are placed in strategic locations depending upon the climate. Vapor-impermeable membranes called "sill gaskets," also known as termite shields, are generally placed on top of the foundation to prevent moisture from wicking into the framed wall.

Rain, especially wind-driven rain, can cause moisture problems in walls. To control moisture, builders and contractors generally incorporate control measures such as flashing, caulking, and weatherstripping around windows, doors, and bottom plates.[41]

Mold

Excess moisture in the home can result in the growth of mold. Molds are part of the natural environment—and in the outdoors, molds break down organic matter such as fallen leaves and dead trees. Indoors, however, mold growth should be avoided. Molds reproduce by means of tiny spores that are invisible to the naked eye and float through both outdoor and indoor air. When mold spores land on indoor surfaces that are wet, mold begins growing indoors.

There are many types of mold, and none of them will grow without water or moisture. Allergic reactions to mold are common and can occur immediately or be delayed. Mold exposure can be harmful to people with asthma, and can irritate the eyes, skin, nose, throat, and lungs of both mold-allergic and non-allergic people.[42]

Windows

Energy-efficient windows, also called high-performance windows, are necessary for optimum thermal enclosure. Energy-efficient windows protect the inside of the home from the sun's heat and ultraviolet (UV) rays in the summer, and they prevent heat from escaping during the winter. Windows must be properly installed, and any spaces between the window frame and wall framing must be sealed.

Double-paned windows are made with two layers of glass and are also known as double-glazed. The glass panes are spaced apart and hermetically sealed, leaving an insulating air space. Triple-paned windows are recommended in areas with extreme climates, and windows are now available with as many as four of five panes.

Gas-filled spacers minimize heat transfer. "Low-emissivity" coatings, referred to as "low-e," are microscopically thin, virtually invisible, metal or metallic oxide layers that are deposited directly on the surface of one or more panes of glass in a window. Vacuum-insulated glass is also available.

> **"Heat gain" and "heat loss" through windows are responsible for 25 to 30% of residential heating and cooling energy use.[43]**
>
> —U.S. Department of Energy

U-Factor

U-Factor measures the rate of heat transfer through a product, and is a criterion used for measuring the energy performance of a window. The U-Factor represents two things—heat loss during cold weather, and heat gain during warm weather. U-Factor values range from 0.20 to 1.20. The lower the number, the better the window is able to provide insulation.

The National Fenestration Rating Council (NFRC) operates a voluntary program that tests, certifies, and labels windows, doors, and skylights based on their energy performance ratings.[44]

The Solar Heat Gain Coefficient (SHGC) measures how much of the sun's heat comes through a window. Values range from 0 to 1. The lower the number, the less solar heat that comes through the window.

"Visible transmittance" (VT) is the amount of light emitted. A high VT number will maximize daylight. "Air leakage" is the rate of air movement around a window. The NFRC label is shown below, along with infographics added by the author.

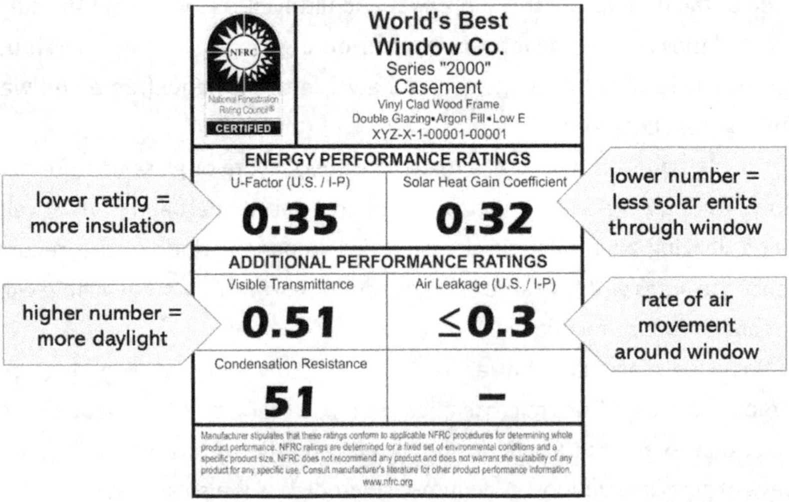

Awnings

Awnings can be installed to shade a window from the sun's heat and glare. According to the U.S. Department of Energy, window awnings can reduce solar heat gain in the summer by up to 65% on south-facing windows and 77% on west-facing windows.[45] Awnings require ventilation to keep hot air from becoming trapped around the window, generally controlled by vents. Retractable awnings can be closed during the winter, which saves energy since sunlight will emit through the window and help warm the house. Conversely, non-retractable awnings can increase energy use in the winter, unless they are positioned in such a way to allow sunlight.

Solar Screens

Solar screens can reduce solar heat gain, ultraviolet (UV) damage, and glare. Screens can be installed on the interior or exterior as roller shades or fixed panels, and they typically allow for a view out the window as well as light transmission. Solar screens look similar to traditional window screens but provide more efficiency benefits. Benefits vary based on the level of openness, visibility, and light transmission.[46]

Doors

Exterior doors are available with energy-efficient features. Common types include doors with a steel skin with a polyurethane foam insulation core. Generally, there is a magnetic strip that serves as weatherstripping. Doors also have R-values, typically ranging from R-5 to R-6 without a window. High-performance doors are available with triple-weather seals, multi-point locking, and triple-pane windows.

Doors also have performance ratings from the National Fenestration Rating Council (NFRC). The label shows the Solar Heat Gain Coefficient (SHGC) and U-Factor. Some models of glass or patio doors are made with layers of glass, low-emissivity (low-e) coatings, and/or low-conductivity gases between the glass panes. Storm doors made of aluminum, steel, fiberglass, or wood may have foam insulation inside their frames. Other models may have low-emissivity glass or glazing.[47]

BLUEPRINT #3

Heating, Ventilation, and Air Conditioning

Heating, ventilation, and air conditioning systems are commonly referred to as "HVAC." Systems that operate through the entire home are called "central" heating or air conditioning. Proper sizing of equipment is essential, since incorrect HVAC sizing can reduce overall effectiveness, cause stress on system components, and lead to poor humidity control. HVAC requirements are measured in British Thermal Units (BTUs) and based on the following factors:

- Geographic location of the home
- Home orientation (north, south, east, or west)
- House size in square feet of living space
- Window types, and where located
- Insulation

Requirements may also be measured in Gigajoules (GJ) and kilowatt hours (kWh). High-performance HVAC systems are based on measurable results and encompass a whole house approach. Heating and cooling efficiency is optimized when homes are equipped with proper ventilation, energy-efficient windows, adequate insulation, and air sealing. Using a programmable thermostat and ceiling fans also help maximize HVAC efficiency.

HVAC systems are built in accordance with ASHRAE. Founded in 1894 as the American Society of Heating, Refrigerating, and Air-Conditioning Engineers, ASHRAE standards are utilized in 132 nations. The building codes and home labeling programs featured in this book incorporate ASHRAE energy-efficiency protocols.

Furnaces

Furnaces deliver heat through hot-air ducts. Furnaces are the most common home heating system, and can run on gas, oil, propane, or electricity. Heating fuel efficiency is rated under a program called Annual Fuel Utilization Efficiency (AFUE), which measures the efficiency in converting fuel to energy. Energy-efficient furnaces are generally rated in the 80 to 95% range, and in accordance with the type of fuel, product criteria, and geographic area.[48]

Boilers

Boilers do not use a duct system. Homes are heated through steam or hot water that circulates through radiators, baseboards, or radiant floor systems. Fuel types used in boilers include gas, propane, and oil. Features that can improve boiler efficiency include an electric ignition, which eliminates the need to have the pilot light burning all the time, as well as technologies that extract more heat using the same amount of fuel. Boiler efficiency is also measured using the Annual Fuel Utilization Efficiency (AFUE) system.

Hot-Water Radiators

Hot-water radiators are one of the most common heat distribution systems in newer homes, second only to forced-air systems. They are typically a baseboard-type radiator or an upright design that resembles steam radiators. To optimize energy efficiency in hot-water radiators, the system can be retrofitted to provide additional settings to control heat in different areas of the home.

"Automatic valves" can be installed that are regulated by thermostats in each zone. To prevent water pipes from freezing, temperatures must be set to the lowest point recommended for the local climate, including zones within the home that are infrequently used.[49]

Steam Radiators

Steam heating is one of the oldest centralized heating methods and it is often found in older homes. Because the process involves boiling and condensing water, steam is less efficient, and there are often lag times between turning the boiler on and heat availability.

The plumbing infrastructure of steam systems is somewhat challenging for energy-efficient retrofit projects. There are a few steps you can take to prevent heat loss, such as installing "heat reflectors" behind the radiators. Reflectors can be especially helpful if the outside walls are poorly insulated. The best strategy is to consult with a heating specialist regarding cleaning, maintenance, and replacement of vents, valves, and steam traps to maintain maximum comfort.[50]

Ductless Systems

Energy-efficient heating and/or cooling systems are available for homes that cannot accommodate ductwork. Ductless systems are known as "mini-splits" and typically include a number of indoor units for each room or climate area, an outdoor unit, and connecting refrigerant lines. Both heating and cooling functions are generated through a heat pump. Common applications for ductless systems include homes with electric heat, or older homes that have radiators or baseboard heat. Ductless systems are often used to conserve energy in rooms that are not regularly occupied.[51]

Heat Pumps

Heat pumps offer an energy-efficient alternative to furnaces and air conditioners. Products operate the same way as refrigerators, making the cool space cooler and the warm space warmer. "Air-source heat pumps" (ASHP) have been used for many years in nearly all parts of the United States.

Until recently they have not been used in areas with extended periods of subfreezing temperatures. However, in recent years, air-source heat pump technology has advanced so that it now offers a legitimate space heating alternative in colder regions. Natural Resources Canada completed a study that found that air-source heat pumps work well in Canadian winters based on testing completed in Ontario.[52]

> **An air-source heat pump can deliver one-and-a-half to three times more heat energy to a home than the electrical energy it consumes. This is because a heat pump moves heat rather than converting it from a fuel.[53]**
>
> —U.S. Department of Energy

"Ground-source heat pumps" (GSHP) extract heat from the ground with buried plastic pipe. The below-grade ground temperature is constant and improves the system's efficiency. Heat is removed from the ground in winter for space heating. In the summer, heat is removed back to the ground to cool the home. "Water source pumps" operate similarly to ground-source systems, but they extract heat from a body of water that is cycled through pipes from nearby lakes or reservoirs. Heat is collected from water and delivered to heat or cool the inside.

"Absorption" heat pumps can be driven by gas, propane, solar-heated water, or geothermal heated water. Because gas is the predominant energy source, these products are also referred to as gas-fired heat pumps.

The chart below lists a number of heating systems that can be used to heat an entire home or provide a supplemental source of heat. Information is adapted from the U.S. Department of Energy.[54]

Alternative Types of Heating	
Wood Stoves	Wood stoves are typically made of cast iron, steel, or stone and generate heat from split logs, known as cordwood. EPA-certified stoves are cleaner burning and more energy efficient.
Pellet Stoves	Pellet stoves are similar in appearance to woodstoves and need electricity to operate. Pellets made from ground, dried wood and biomass wastes are poured into a hopper. Corn kernels can be used in lieu of pellets.
Forced Air Furnaces	Also known as warm-air furnaces, units are designed to burn cordwood, wood pellets, or wood chips and can heat an entire residence. Heat is distributed through ducts powered by a blower fan.
Fireplaces	Traditional masonry fireplaces are built with brick or stone. Low-mass fireplaces are engineered and prefabricated in a manufacturing facility prior to installation. Most fireplaces are not used as a primary source of heat.
Fireplace Inserts	Units are installed within the firebox of an existing metal or masonry fireplace. Similar in function to free-standing wood burning stoves. EPA-certified models are less polluting and more efficient.
Fireplace Retrofits	A fireplace retrofit is a device that is installed into an existing wood-burning fireplace to help reduce smoke pollution. They can be installed in masonry or factory-built fireplaces.
Gas & Propane Stoves	Stoves can burn either natural gas or propane, and are typically very energy efficient. They emit very little pollution, require little maintenance, and can be installed almost anywhere in the home. They can be vented through an existing chimney or through a wall. The EPA supports models that vent outside.

Ventilation

"Whole-house ventilation" systems deliver controlled, uniform ventilation throughout the entire home. Systems can use one or more fans within the home's ductwork system to exhaust stale air from the house, and/or supply fresh air into the house.

Air filtration and ventilation help to control moisture, reduce indoor air pollutants, and alleviate common household problems. Ventilation systems are constantly working and continuously exchange indoor air with outdoor air to control airborne pollutants.

An important function of the home ventilation system is that air leakage is controlled through strategically placed "intentional" vents. As explained earlier in the thermal enclosure section, the home must be well-sealed so that the air cooled by an air conditioning system—and/or the air warmed by a heating system—does not escape.

Types of Ventilation Systems
EXHAUST VENTILATION Systems work by depressurizing the building, typically with one fan connected to a centrally located exhaust point in the house.
SUPPLY VENTILATION Systems work by pressurizing the building, forcing outside air into the home, while the inside air exits through various vents.
BALANCED VENTILATION Systems neither pressurize nor depressurize a house. Instead, they introduce and exhaust equal quantities of fresh outside air and polluted inside air.
ENERGY RECOVERY VENTILATION Systems provide controlled ventilation while minimizing energy loss and maintaining constant temperatures and humidity.

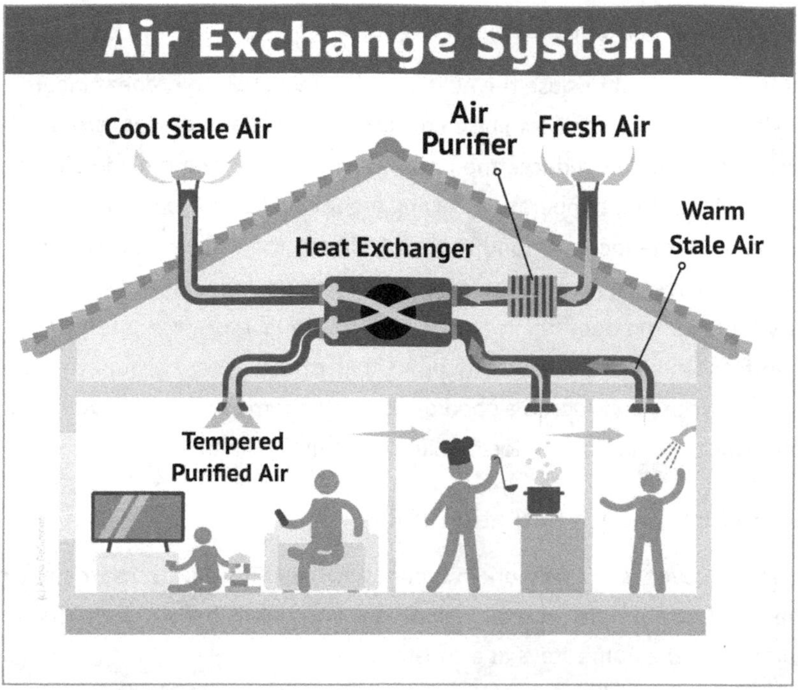

Mechanical Air Exchange Systems

Because energy-efficient homes are built to a higher standard of air tightness, mechanical ventilation is recommended for a number of reasons. Drafty old homes lose a lot of heat—but they also let in healthy fresh air. According to Health Canada, mechanical ventilation systems provide three important benefits: [55]

- They provide oxygen for occupants since people deplete oxygen as they breathe.
- They remove contaminants that are emitted by people and certain building materials.
- They remove excess humidity, which ensures building durability and efficiency in heating, and helps prevent mold and mildew.

Considered an essential component of high-performance HVAC systems, mechanical air exchange systems are comprised of two types: heat recovery ventilation and energy recovery ventilation. Each type is described below.

Heat Recovery Ventilation (HRV)

Heat recovery systems use the heat in stale exhaust air to preheat incoming fresh air. The cold, dry incoming air absorbs this heat as it passes through the exchange unit. This reduces the energy required to bring outside air up to the ambient room temperature, saving money on heating bills.

Because the incoming and outgoing air are traveling in separate channels, air sources never mix. This approach is known as counterflow. Although HRVs require the operation of a fan on a continual basis, the energy recovered from the inside air is many times that of the energy required for the fan.[56] HRVs are considered a good option if the home does not have air conditioning, or if the home is located in a less-humid climate.

Energy Recovery Ventilation (ERV)

Energy recovery systems work in similar ways as HRVs, but transfer some of the moisture from the outgoing airstream into the incoming air so that the humidity in the home stays at a constant level.

In cold winter climates, ERV systems transfer humidity from the air being extracted to the incoming outdoor (and dry) air to help keep the ambient internal humidity at a reasonable level at all times. In the summer, the humidity transfer reverses and the humidity in outside air is removed before it is injected into the home.[57] ERVs are considered a good option if the home has air conditioning and the home is located in a humid climate.

Fans

"Whole-house fans" provide excellent ventilation to help lower indoor temperatures, and in most climates, they can serve as a substitute for an air conditioner. When combined with ceiling fans, whole house fans help deliver more comfort in hot weather. Fans can be installed with or without ductwork, and are generally installed in an attic, with a roof-mounted vent.[58]

Fans are the least expensive and most energy-efficient way to cool a home, and work well when combined with other heating or cooling methods. "Spot ventilation" fans are used in strategic places such as bathrooms and kitchens—and vented outside.

Ceiling fans re-circulate air and can be used on a year-round basis. High-volume, low-speed fans (HVLS) are more aerodynamic and can move large volumes of air while delivering more comfort.

In the summer, ceiling fans should be operated *counterclockwise* so that the airflow is pushed downward, creating a cooling effect. In the winter, fans should turn in a *clockwise* direction, which sends the heat in a downward direction.

> **Ceiling fans cool people—not rooms. To save energy, turn off the ceiling fan when the room is not occupied.**[59]
>
> —Energy Star

Duct Cleaning

Air ducts in the home can harbor particles of dust, pollen, or other debris. If moisture is present, the potential for mold growth increases, and spores are released into the living areas.

Air duct cleaning is performed by a team of professionals who will remove the grills in front of each vent. A special long hose is connected to a high-powered vacuum cleaner that extracts the contents and sends it to a truck parked outside your home. The service provider may suggest the application of "biocides" into the ductwork to kill microbiological contaminants. Some duct cleaners have small robots with rotating brushes that provide a more thorough cleaning.

If you have furry pets, frequently use a fireplace or wood (or pellet) burning stove, or there are smokers in your household, it's a good idea to schedule duct cleaning every few years.

Indoor Air Quality

The primary cause of indoor air quality problems stems from pollution sources that release gases or particles into the air inside the home. Also, high temperatures and humidity levels can increase the concentration of some pollutants.

Pollutants consist of "particulate matter (PM)." PMs represent a mixture of solid particles and liquid droplets found in the air. Some particles, such as dust, dirt, soot, or smoke, are large or dark enough to be seen with the naked eye. Others are so small they can only be detected using an electron microscope.

There are two types of PMs: "fine particulate matter," which is up to 2.5 micrometers in diameter, and "coarse particulate matter," which is up to 10 micrometers in diameter. The average human hair is about 70 micrometers in diameter, making it 30 times larger than the fine particle. The two types may also be referred to as "fine" and "ultrafine."

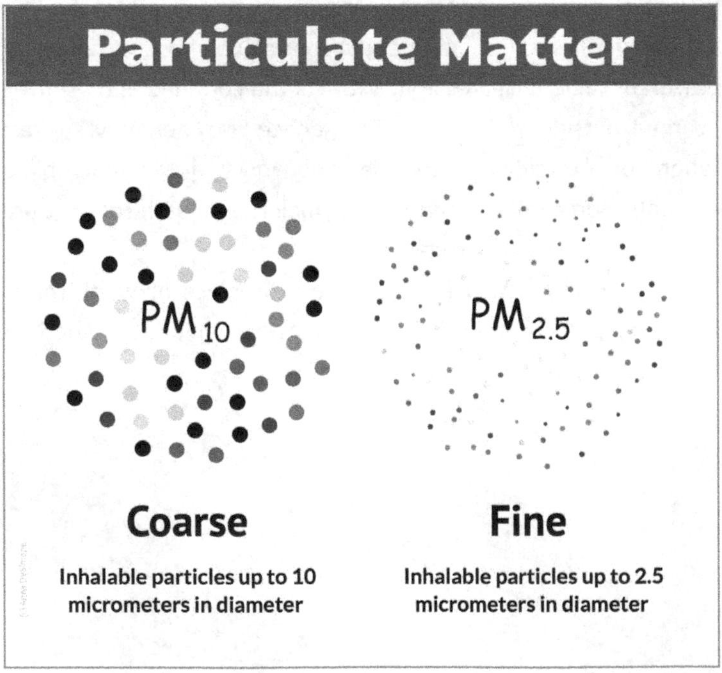

PMs originate from indoor sources and outside sources that migrate into the home. Examples of indoor sources are cooking, burning of candles, cigarette smoking, and unvented fireplaces or space heaters. Examples of outdoor sources are construction sites, unpaved roads, fields, smokestacks, and fires.

Outdoor PMs are also generated from the atmosphere as a result of complex reactions of chemicals and pollutants emitted from power plants, industries, and automobiles.[60]

Management of indoor air quality requires circulation and ventilation. If ventilation is not adequate, pollutant levels can increase in two ways:

- by not bringing in enough fresh outdoor air to dilute emissions from indoor sources, and
- by not carrying indoor air pollutants out of the home.

The most effective solution to improve indoor air quality in your home involves removing or reducing the sources of pollutants and ventilating or exchanging indoor air with clean outdoor air.

This objective can be facilitated through a whole-house air filtering system that is integrated with the home's furnace or HVAC system. Portable air cleaners can reduce indoor air pollution; however, they cannot remove every type of pollutant.[61]

There are many shapes and sizes of air filters. "Flat" filters are matted, with densely packed fibers. "Pleated," accordion-like filters are constructed with similar matted fibers. "Media" filters are accordion-like units of filtration media, typically at least 8 inches thick.

Below is a chart listing the most common types of air cleaning filters and efficiency ratings used in HVAC systems and air purification appliances.

Types of Air Cleaning Filters

HEPA

High Efficiency Particulate Air (HEPA) are filters made of various synthetic fibers. HEPA filters block out 99.97% of all particles 0.3 micrometers or larger and capture about 80% of indoor particles.

ULPA

Ultra-Low Penetration Air (ULPA) is a new filter technology that blocks 99.99% of particles measuring 0.12 micrometers—much smaller than the HEPA threshold. ULPA may restrict air flow, therefore cleaning less air.

ELECTRONIC

Electronic filters are sometimes called electrostatic precipitators. A high-voltage current puts an electrical charge on particles as air passes through. A charged collector plate traps the particles at the opposite end of the unit. Filters may be inserted into ductwork.

ULTRAVIOLET

Components of ultraviolet (UV) radiation are built into the filtering system to extinguish airborne pollutants such as mold, fungus, and bacteria. UV filters can be installed alongside an electrostatic system.

Efficiency Rating Systems

CADR

Clean Air Delivery Rate (CADR) is a measure of the amount of contaminant-free air delivered by a room air cleaner. Energy Star products require CADR testing.

MERV

Minimum Efficiency Reporting Value (MERV) is a rating system that provides an overall value of effectiveness of an air filter on a 16-point scale. Residential home products are generally within the 6 to 12 range.

MPR

The micro-particle performance rating (MPR) is a system that was developed by 3M which rates the manufacturer's filters and ability to capture airborne particles smaller than 1 micron.

FPR

Filter performance ratings (FPR) are similar to MERV and based on a number scale of 4 through 10. Designed by Home Depot, FPR assesses brands sold in stores, including Honeywell.

EPA Indoor airPLUS

The Environmental Protection Agency has a voluntary partnership and labeling program called *EPA Indoor airPLUS*. The EPA created *Indoor airPLUS* to help builders meet the growing consumer preference for homes with improved indoor air quality. *Indoor airPLUS* builds on the foundation of the EPA's Energy Star requirements for new homes.

The builder must first design a home to earn the Energy Star certified home label, and then add additional home design and construction features to help protect qualified homes from moisture and mold, pests, and combustion gases and other airborne pollutants.

Before the home officially earns the *Indoor airPLUS* label, it is inspected by an independent third-party to ensure compliance with the EPA's guidelines and specifications.

Resources:

EPA Indoor Air Plus Program
www.epa.gov/indoorairplus

EPA Indoor Air Quality
www.epa.gov/indoor-air-quality-iaq

Canada Residential Indoor Air Quality Guidelines
www.canada.ca/en/health-canada/services/air-quality/residential-indoor-air-quality-guidelines.html

Air Conditioning

Most residential central air conditioners are called "split-systems" because they have both outdoor and indoor components. The evaporator coil is attached to the furnace inside the home. The condenser and compressor are installed outside.

Air conditioners are rated according to the "Seasonal Energy Efficiency Ratio (SEER)" and "Energy Efficiency Ratio (EER)." SEER measures how efficiently a cooling system will operate over an entire season. EER measures how efficiently a cooling system will operate when the outdoor temperature is at a specific level, such as 95 degrees Fahrenheit.[62]

SEER ratings were created so that consumers could compare the cooling costs of different air conditioners over one-, five-, ten-, and fifteen-year time periods. Factors are based on the air conditioner's size, local cost of electricity per kilowatt-hour (kWh), and the annual cooling hours for your location as estimated by the Environmental Protection Agency.[63]

Ductless Mini-split Air Conditioners

Mini-splits are small-size systems that offer flexibility for heating and cooling individual rooms, each with its own thermostat. Since mini-splits have no ducts, they avoid the energy losses associated with the ductwork of central forced-air systems. The outdoor unit can be located as far away as 50 feet from the indoor evaporator. The indoor air handlers can be suspended from a ceiling, mounted flush into a drop ceiling, or hung on a wall. Floor-standing models are also available. Unlike window units, they are installed with only a small hole in the wall.

Room Air Conditioners

Room-size air conditioners have significantly advanced in recent years, and models now have energy-saving features. Air conditioners with "connected functionality" allow users to adjust settings using smart home technology. Products are available that are "smart-grid ready," allowing users to take advantage of cost-saving programs offered by a utility company.

Evaporative Coolers

Evaporative coolers are suitable for geographic areas that have low humidity. Water is evaporated into the air, providing a natural and energy-efficient means of cooling. Products are also known as "swamp coolers." They can be connected to ductwork to cool a number of rooms. Floor-standing, portable devices will cool an entire room or section of the home.

When operating an evaporative cooler, windows are opened part way to allow warm indoor air to escape as it is replaced by cooled air. Unlike central air conditioning systems that recirculate the same air, evaporative coolers provide a steady stream of outdoor air into the house. According to the Department of Energy, systems cost about half as much as central air conditioning systems and use about one-quarter as much energy.[64]

Programmable Thermostats

Advanced scheduling of air temperatures can save a significant amount of money. Programmable devices are effective for reducing energy costs to heat the home in the winter—or cool the home in the summer.

Basic features allow homeowners to schedule settings for each HVAC zone in the home for different days and times. More advanced features include voice-activation, mobile apps, email alerts, and other reminders. Popular models include Google Nest, Ecobee, Comfort, Johnson Controls GLAS, Heagstat, Orbit, Lux, and several types from Honeywell.

Sophisticated devices include sensors that monitor outdoor temperatures, humidity levels, and automatically adjust settings. A "changeover" feature automatically switches the system from heating to cooling as the weather changes. When you're on your way home from work, based on your mobile phone's location, the *Honeywell Lyric* starts warming or cooling your house when you are 10 miles away.

Some utility companies offer free programmable thermostats to their customers during special promotions or with the purchase of certain appliances.

BLUEPRINT #4

Lighting and Appliances

The U.S. Environmental Protection Agency established the Energy Star program in 1992. To date, the program and its partners helped American families save more than 4 trillion kilowatt-hours of electricity and achieve over 3.5 billion metric tons of greenhouse gas reductions.[65]

Energy Star Canada is a voluntary partnership between the government of Canada and industry to make high-efficiency products readily available and visible to Canadians. The program was initiated in 2001 and is administered by Natural Resources Canada.[66]

> **Lighting and appliances in your home come with two price tags—the purchase price and cost to operate and maintain them.**[67]
>
> —Energy Star

Lighting

Light bulbs and fixtures are now available that use 70 to 90% less energy than traditional models. New types of bulbs and fixtures can last up to 15 times longer than traditional incandescent light bulbs.

LED stands for light emitting diode. LED lighting products produce light up to 90% more efficiently than incandescent light bulbs. Incandescent bulbs produce light using electricity to heat a metal filament until it becomes “white” hot or is said to incandesce. As a result, incandescent bulbs release 90% of their energy as heat.

Energy Star LED bulbs are subject to very specific requirements designed to replicate the experience of a standard bulb and can be used for a wide variety of applications. LEDs are “directional” light sources, which means they emit light in a specific direction, and are able to use light and energy more efficiently in a multitude of applications.[68]

Manufacturers and utility companies sometimes give homeowners free LED bulbs in conjunction with product promotions.

Appliances

Energy Star has certified approximately 70,000 products based on its energy-efficiency criteria. Builders throughout the U.S. and Canada offer Energy Star products in their energy-efficient home models. Products include furnaces, boilers, heat pumps, heating, ventilation systems, fans, air conditioners, and the full range of household appliances and lighting. The chart below highlights recent advancements in the performance of premium products with the Energy Star label.[69]

Appliance	Performance
Refrigerators	New models operate more quietly, and redesigned doors provide better insulation to keep food fresher, and with about 9% more efficiency.
Dishwashers	Smart features provide more effective and quieter operation and minimize water use. Energy efficiency is about 12% greater than conventional units.
Clothes Washers	New models utilize 45% less water and 25% less energy than standard washers.
Ceiling Fans	New models move air 50% more efficiently than conventional fans while providing the same amount of cooling.
Ventilation Fans	Products now include high-performance motors and improved blade designs, using 50% less energy.

Find an Energy Star Product in the U.S.
https://www.energystar.gov/productfinder/?s=mega

Find an Energy Star Product in Canada
https://www.nrcan.gc.ca/energy-efficiency/energy-star-canada/energy-star-products/12519

BLUEPRINT #5

Water Management

Our final blueprint encompasses one of the most important aspects of our lives—water. There are three imperatives covered: efficient hot water heating; water conservation; and water safety.

Efficient Water Heating

There are a number of innovative hot-water heating options that use less energy, save money, and provide a household with sufficient hot water. Conventional storage water heaters remain the most popular type of water heating system. Single-family storage water heaters generally include a "ready reservoir," which holds anywhere from 20 to 80 gallons of water. Hot water is released from the top of the tank, and as water is used, cold water enters the bottom of the tank, ensuring the tank is always full. Tanks are usually heavily insulated, and the recommended thermal resistance (R-value) ranges from R-12 to R-25.

"Tankless" water heaters, also known as "demand" or "tankless coil" heaters, do not require a storage tank. When a hot water tap is turned on, water is heated as it flows through a heating coil or heat exchanger installed on the main furnace or boiler. Tankless coil water heaters are most efficient during cold months when the home heating system is used regularly. Conversely, these systems are less efficient in warmer climates.

"Heat pump" water heaters use electricity to move heat from one place to another instead of generating heat directly. Heaters can be installed as a stand-alone system or in combination with the home's space heating system. They work best in moderate climates and can also be retrofitted to work with an existing conventional storage water heater.[70]

> Heat pump water heaters have shown to be two–to three–times more efficient than conventional electric water heaters.
>
> —U.S. Department of Energy

Solar Hot Water Heating

Solar hot water heating is a great way to heat your hot water for free. Systems include insulated storage tanks and solar collectors. The two types of solar water heating systems are "active" and "passive."

With an active system, "direct pumps" circulate household water through collectors. These systems work well in moderate climates. In colder climates, systems utilize "indirect pumps," which circulate non-freezing "heat transfer fluid" through the collectors and a heat exchanger. This process heats the water that flows into the home.

Passive systems include "integral collector-storage," which work well in moderate climates. The second passive type is "thermosyphon," which requires storage tanks be located above the collectors so that warm water rises to them. Roofs must be able to handle their weight.

Water Conservation

According to the Environmental Protection Agency, each American uses an average of 88 gallons of water a day at home. At least 20% less water can be used by installing water-efficient fixtures and appliances.[71]

"Water re-use," also known as "water recycling," reclaims water from a variety of sources. Water undergoes a treatment process and is then re-used for other purposes such as landscape irrigation. Water re-use can provide alternatives to existing water supplies and can be used to enhance water security, sustainability, and resilience.[72]

"Grey water" consists of water that is directed from sinks, showers, bathtubs, washing machines, and dishwashers. Water sourced from these household fixtures is considered safe to handle and is generally treated for re-use for landscape irrigation, toilet flushing, and other household uses.

"Rainwater recovery" systems capture rainwater from the roof of the home and redirect it to a storage tank. This water can be used for irrigating the landscape, watering vegetable gardens, and other outdoor purposes.

"Rainwater collectors" are available with varying degrees of functionality, including models that connect to bathroom fixtures.

EPA WaterSense

WaterSense is a program administered by the EPA that makes it easier for consumers to choose products that will help the environment. Products with the WaterSense label include sinks, faucets, toilets, showerheads, and lawn irrigation products.

WaterSense-labeled homes offer homebuyers a whole-house solution to help save water, energy, and money while maintaining a high level of performance.[73] Some of the benefits of WaterSense-labeled homes include:

- Faster hot water delivery
- No visible leaks
- Independently certified fixtures that use less water and perform as well or better than standard models
- Outdoor irrigation that is low-maintenance, water-efficient, and that offers high-performance

Resources:

WaterSense-labeled Homes
https://www.epa.gov/watersense/watersense-labeled-homes

WaterSense – Product Search
https://lookforwatersense.epa.gov

WaterSense – Find a Rebate
https://lookforwatersense.epa.gov/Rebate-Finder.html

Water Safety

Congress passed the Safe Drinking Water Act (SDWA) in 1974 to protect public health by regulating the nation's public drinking water supply. The SDWA regulates many laws to protect drinking water and its sources, including rivers, lakes, reservoirs, springs, and groundwater wells.

Private wells that serve fewer than 25 individuals are excluded from SDWA regulation. SDWA authorizes the Environmental Protection Agency to set national health-based standards for drinking water to protect against both naturally occurring and human-made contaminants.

The National Primary Drinking Water Regulations (NPDWRs) oversee the legally enforceable standards that apply to public water systems. Primary standards and treatment techniques protect consumers by limiting the levels of contaminants in drinking water.[74]

Most people in the United States receive water from a community water system that provides its customers with an annual water quality report, also known as a *Consumer Confidence Report*. The report contains information on contaminants found, possible health effects, and the water's source.

Private Drinking Water Wells

According to the Environmental Protection Agency, an estimated 13 million households rely on private wells for drinking water in the United States. The EPA does not regulate private wells, nor does it provide recommended criteria or standards for individual wells. Private well owners are responsible for the safety of their water.[75]

If you have a private drinking water supply, the EPA recommends that water be tested annually for total coliform bacteria, nitrates, total dissolved solids, and pH levels. Testing is especially important if you have a new well, or have replaced or repaired pipes, pumps, or the well casing. If anyone in your household is having recurring gastro-intestinal illness, order a coliform bacteria test immediately. Every three years, testing should be completed for sulfate, chloride, iron, and manganese.

If you are expecting a new baby in the household, have your well tested for nitrates before the baby is brought home—and then again within six months. The best time to test for nitrate is during the spring or summer following rain.

Water can be tested for chloride and sodium if your water tastes salty, and tested for hydrogen sulfide or metals if your water has an objectionable taste or smell. Volatile organic compounds (VOCs) testing is recommended if there have been any spills or leaks from chemicals or fuels near your water supply.[76]

Most county health departments provide assistance for testing bacteria or nitrates. If you can't find a state-certified laboratory in your area, you can call the *Safe Drinking Water Hotline* at 800-426-4791 or visit: https://www.epa.gov/ground-water-and-drinking-water/safe-drinking-water-information

Find a certified water testing laboratory in the U.S.
www.epa.gov/dwlabcert/contact-information-certification-programs-and-certified-laboratories-drinking-water

Tap Score
Easy home water testing and reporting from *Simple Lab*, an award-winning science and health services company founded at the University of California in Berkeley, offers testing for city water, well water, and specialized testing. www.mytapscore.com

Canada

Health Canada's Water and Air Quality Bureau develops the *Guidelines for Canadian Drinking Water Quality* in partnership with the provinces, territories, and other federal departments. Guidelines are used by every jurisdiction in Canada and serve as the basis for establishing drinking water quality requirements for all Canadians.

Health Canada participates in the development of the World Health Organization (WHO) guidelines for drinking water. The Canada Bureau also works closely and shares information with other government agencies such as the U.S. Environmental Protection Agency.[77]

Health Canada Program, "Be Well Aware – Test Your Well Water"

Health Canada's Water Quality Division recommends water-quality testing every two years, or more often if changes in taste, smell, or color are noticed. More frequent testing is advised if there are any concerns about coliforms or *E. coli.* Water should be tested if there are recent activities or land-use changes near the well. Shallow wells, or wells that have only a thin layer of soil over rock can become contaminated and should be tested more often.

The local public health unit in your province may recommend testing of other chemicals that can affect health. Generalized water quality tests help determine what types of water treatment devices may be needed, or if there are conditions that could potentially cause problems.

The best times to sample your well water are in early spring just after the thaw, after a long dry spell, following heavy rains, or after not using it for a long time. Following are recommendations:

- Check the well cap regularly to ensure that it is securely in place and watertight.
- Run the cold water tap for a few minutes each morning or when the system has not been used for a number of hours. Use only cold tap water for drinking, cooking, and making baby formula.
- During boil-water advisories or boil-water orders, bring water to a rolling boil for a full minute for all water used for drinking, cooking, washing fruits and vegetables, and brushing your teeth.

The above information was adapted from Health Canada's *Be Well Aware*[78] publication, which is available at: www.canada.ca/en/health-canada

Canada Water Quality

www.canada.ca/en/health-canada/topics/health-environment/water-quality-health.html

SGS Water Testing in Canada

Home water testing services with offices located in all provinces.
www.sgs.ca/en/solutions/quality-water-testing-in-canada

CHAPTER 3

Renewable Energy

USING RENEWABLE ENERGY REDUCES THE USE OF FOSSIL FUELS, the largest sources of carbon dioxide emissions. Also referred to as "clean energy," renewable energy comes from naturally replenishing sources. The priority to reduce greenhouse gas emissions is highly dependent upon the use of clean and renewable sources of energy.

According to the U.S. Energy Information Administration (EIA), until the mid-1800s, wood was the source of nearly all of the nation's energy needs for heating, cooking, and lighting. From the late 1800s until today, the major sources of energy have been from three fossil fuels—coal, petroleum, and natural gas.

The EIA further states that until the 1900s, the most-used renewable energy sources in the United States were wood and hydropower. Since then, energy consumption from each of the following sources has increased: solar energy, biofuels, geothermal, and wind energy. Over the past 11 years, the consumption of biofuels, geothermal, solar, and wind energy in the United States has tripled.[79]

This chapter explains the infrastructure and financial incentives available to homeowners, and features the following renewable energy sources: Solar Energy, Geothermal, Wind, Hydroelectric, and Biomass. Consumption for each of these types of energy is noted in the chart below.

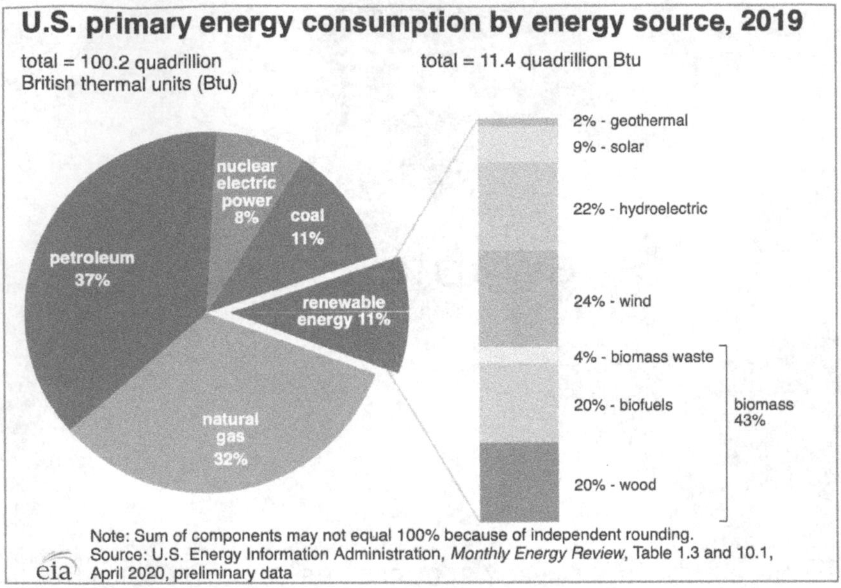

Source: U.S. Energy Information Administration

As a residential homeowner, your renewable energy will be derived from a natural source. Therefore, it needs to be available where you live—and it needs to produce a worthwhile supply to cover your investment. Your energy potential will depend upon factors such as the number of daylight hours from the sun, wind patterns, or the flow rate of water from a private stream.

Geothermal energy is not available in all geographic areas. However, new sites are in development throughout the U.S. and Canada. No matter what type of renewable energy you choose, the system needs to be properly sized and installed in order to meet your household needs.

Grid-tied Connectivity

Most renewable systems installed in residential homes have a "grid-tied" connection with their utility company. Grid connections are two-way connections. Electricity generated by your system is stored on the grid. After that energy is depleted, the system switches over—drawing electricity from the utility company. "Off the grid" systems are solely dependent upon a renewable source for power. High-capacity batteries can provide extended power to both off-grid or grid-tied systems.

Energy produced by your system is called "site energy," and the energy drawn from the grid is called "source energy." When a site system produces more energy than the house consumes within a billing cycle, this outcome is known as "excess generation."

When choosing a renewable energy system, consider that your equipment needs are based on the home's square footage and average electricity use. According to the U.S. Energy Information Administration (EIA), in 2020 the average monthly energy consumption for a U.S. residential household was 909 kilowatt-hours (kWh).[80] Canadian households have similar consumption rates, when averaged across all provinces.[81,82]

Net Metering

Net metering is a compensation structure designed for consumers to receive fair and equitable payment for producing their own energy. Energy use is measured in kilowatt-hours (kWh), and tracked in monthly billing cycles.

Each month, your utility bill will state the number of kilowatt-hours of energy your system produced—and stipulate in dollars and cents the value of that energy. The bill will also state how many kilowatt-hours were drawn from the grid—and stipulate in dollars and cents what you are being charged for that energy. Dollar values for each type of charge can be different, and there may be variances based on peak or non-peak hours.

As a general rule, your compensation for the energy you produce will be given in the form of credits. If you are producing the same amount of energy that you take from the grid—you are effectively operating at little or no cost. Credit values are typically based on either the "full retail electricity rate" or the "avoided cost rate." Compensation plans are based on type of renewable energy and other factors that may be related to state or provincial law.

Most U.S. states and Canadian provinces allow net metering, and general laws often include a number of rules and stipulations. For example, there may be a mandatory requirement that utility companies compensate customers at the full retail rate. In lieu of net metering, some states have established laws for alternative programs such as "net billing," explained below.

Net Billing

The main difference between net metering and net billing is that different rates are used to value the energy. With net billing, customers pay full retail price when they use energy from the grid—but get paid a wholesale price when they sell it back. Other aspects of the customer agreement are very similar to net metering plans.

When comparing net billing or net metering programs, consider all options and take financial incentives into account. Other options that can make a difference in your overall costs include eligibility to be charged discounted rates during off-peak hours.

Renewable Energy Certificates (RECs)

Renewable energy certificates are issued when one megawatt-hour (MWh) of electricity is generated and delivered to your electricity grid from a renewable energy source such as solar or wind. A megawatt unit is equal to 1,000 kilowatts (kW). As stated earlier, the monthly average energy consumption is 909 kWh—slightly less than one megawatt. RECs may also be referred to as "renewable energy credits."

RECs play an important role in accounting, tracking, and assigning ownership to renewable electricity generation and use. RECs are commodities that can be traded in compliance markets in states that have renewable portfolio standards (RPS) regulations. Compliance market rules vary by state and fuel type.

As a general rule, homeowners who produce renewable energy own the RECs, which can be sold or traded on the open market. However, in certain situations utility companies retain the ownership rights of the RECs, generally in conjunction with a premium pricing program. Financial entities that administer solar energy leases and power purchase agreements (PPAs) also retain ownership of RECs.

REC tracking and certificate issuing entities cover the whole of the U.S. and Canada, however they are not controlled by any one organization. Specific mechanisms regarding the tracking and trading of RECs are recognized by different levels of governmental entities and state legislation.[83]

Solar Renewable Energy Certificates (SRECs)

SRECs are a type of renewable energy credit that is specifically generated by solar panels and can be sold or traded. As with RECs, legal rights are governed by state or provincial law. Homeowners with solar energy systems in states with SREC markets are able to sell SRECs. States that have established renewable portfolio standards (RPS) regulations may have solar "carve-outs." When a certain percentage of the state's overall renewable energy production must be from a specific source, it is called a carve-out.

Selling Renewable Energy Certificates

In states that have established SREC markets, solar energy system owners can sell their SRECs. The amount of money an owner can receive varies by state, supply and demand, and the state's alternative compliance payment (ACP) program.

According to the national solar energy educational resource and marketplace, Energy Sage, a typical homeowner with a 5-kW solar power system can potentially generate five SRECs per year—worth $200 each. In addition to saving money on their electric bill, the homeowner can pocket an additional $1,000 by selling their SRECs on the open market.[84]

Solar Reviews states that SRECs can be worth as much as $500, depending upon the state, and cites the following examples of SREC market prices on December 31, 2020: $435 in Washington D.C.; $282 in Massachusetts; and $282 in New Jersey.[85]

There are a number of outlets for homeowners to sell their SRECs. You can create an REC and manage your own portfolio with a software program available from SRECTrade. The system allows residential homeowners to create renewable energy certificates, see their REC balance in real-time, and monitor transactions.[86] Learn more at: https://www.srectrade.com/residential

Sol Systems offers a program where homeowners can broker their SRECs. Programs are available in 37 states across the U.S., where solar owners can sell SRECs on the open market or receive an annuity that provides customers a fixed, quarterly payment for each SREC produced—even if the SREC market falls.[87] Learn more at: https://www.solsystems.com

Buying Renewable Energy Certificates

Any person or business can purchase a renewable energy certificate. Known as an "offset," buying an REC is an alternative way to lower your carbon footprint. RECs are sometimes purchased by individuals or companies who want to help reduce greenhouse gas emissions, but are unable to generate their own renewable energy. There are two types of REC buyers—voluntary and compliance.

Voluntary purchases are often made by corporations as part of an overall environmental initiative. For example, grocers and retail stores do not emit GHGs resulting from manufacturing activities. However, emissions from transportation, distribution, and the supply train are factored into the corporate carbon footprint. REC investments provide an offset that reduces the corporate carbon footprint while upholding a strategy for climate action.

Voluntary purchases are made by private individuals who might wish to invest their savings in environmental causes, rather than in stocks and bonds. If the individual does not have a renewable energy system, the REC purchase can be used as an offset to reduce their carbon footprint. However, for homeowners who are operating renewable energy systems, they cannot double-count GHG reductions on both the energy produced and RECs purchased.

Compliance buyers consist of electrical utility companies that must have a certain percent of their electricity generation come from renewable resources. Such obligations are included in the state's renewable portfolio standards (RPS) strategy. When a utility cannot directly generate a sufficient number of RECs, they can purchase them as an offset.

Power Purchase Agreements

Power purchase agreements (PPAs) are financial arrangements in which a third-party developer owns, operates, and maintains the renewable energy system. Solar power purchase agreements are called SPPAs. Under an SPPA, a homeowner agrees to site the system on its property and purchases the system's electric output from the solar services provider for a predetermined period.

The host customer buys the services produced by the PV system rather than the PV system itself. This framework is referred to as the "solar services" model, and the developers who offer SPPAs are known as solar services providers. SPPA arrangements enable the host customer to avoid many of the traditional barriers to the installation of on-site solar systems.[88]

PPAs are available for other types of renewable energy, such as wind or hydroelectric, but mostly in the commercial sector. Due to the strong interest by residential homeowners, leasing and other types of financing programs are expected to increase.

Tax Credits and Deductions

A tax credit is a dollar-for-dollar, bottom-line reduction on your income taxes. Under the U.S. solar investment tax credit (ITC) program, if you purchase and install a solar energy system in 2021 or 2022, you can receive a federal income tax credit of 26%. The credit will be 22% for systems installed in 2023.

Let's say you spend $15,000 on a solar energy system. Your tax credit would be $3,900. When you file your annual tax return, if taxes due are $14,000—that burden drops to $10,100.

If you've prepaid your taxes through payroll deductions, $3,900 will be issued as a refund. Tax credits can be carried forward. If your total taxes are lower than the credit amount, the unused credit can be taken in the following year(s).

Tax credits are also available for completing energy improvements to your home. Qualified improvements include insulation, windows, skylights, exterior doors, and certain types of roofs. Each component must meet specific energy standards, and the IRS provides a calculation worksheet to determine the tax credit.

Deductions are very different from tax credits—they are entered as a line item within the itemized deductions section of your tax return. Deductions effectively shrink your income, whereas tax credits shrink the taxes owed. Many states have issued tax credits (or deductions) to residents who implemented energy improvements to their home or have installed a renewable system.

Local Government Policy

According to *50 States of Solar*, published by the NC Clean Energy Technology Center, from 2015 through 2020, a total of 1,422 policy actions were taken by individual states across the nation.[89]

State and local policies aim to broaden renewable energy use and make it easier for consumers to buy or lease systems. A number of U.S. states and Canadian provinces offer income tax deductions (or credits) for the purchase of renewable energy equipment. Many states have waived sales tax for the purchase of energy-efficient appliances and/or renewable energy technologies and equipment.

A number of U.S. states have issued waivers to property assessment increases resulting from added improvements. Even though the property will increase in value, homeowners are not taxed on the value of energy improvements. Many municipalities have passed ordinances to expedite the processing time for a permit to install a renewable energy system.

Solar and Wind Access Rights

Individual states are issuing state-wide laws at an increasing rate to help support the use of renewable energy. Quite often, state legislature authorizes local counties, cities, and towns to draft ordinances to protect homeowners.

In a growing number of states, homeowners' associations (HOAs) may not prohibit the installation of solar panels. However, most laws also include provisions that allow an HOA to set restrictions regarding the location and placement of panels, as well as limit permissions to owners who own their roof and are responsible for roof maintenance.

A large number of states have issued laws to allow owners of renewable systems to enter into voluntary agreements with their neighbors, providing assurance that no structures will be built that would block the sunlight in the path of their solar energy system. For the most part, states authorize local municipalities to issue ordinances regarding sunlight access, and some states have drafted sample written agreements for cities and towns to distribute to homeowners.

Wind access laws generally pertain to zoning, height of the wind turbine, and required setback from public roads. Approvals for small wind turbine systems can be subject to a variety of approvals. Permits are based on the system size and may be subject to site safety inspections and confirmation of grid access.

Note: Chapter 10, Directory of Rebates and Incentives by State and Province, includes policies regarding net metering, solar/wind access rights, tax credits, and renewable energy certificates.

Power Outage Protection

According to E&E News (Energy and Environment) millions of people lose electrical service each year because of weather-related disruptions. Since 2002, electric companies have reported more than 2,500 major outages to the Department of Energy. Nearly half of the outages were caused by weather conditions—or about 65 weather-related outages per year.[90]

Homeowners with an installed renewable energy system have resources available to protect them against power loss. Although your solar photovoltaic (PV) system or other renewable energy source stores energy on the grid, when the power goes down—your stored energy is not accessible. This is because the grid connection is a two-way connection, and for the safety of the workforce repairing the power lines, all connectivity must be off.

Thanks to the latest development in "power cells," you can store your energy production and effectively operate "off the grid" for an extended period of time. Unlike the traditional back-up generator, which runs on fossil fuels, there are innovative products such as the *Tesla Powerwall, Generac PWRCell, LG Chem, Pika Energy Harbor, Sonnen Eco, Panasonic EverVolt, Nissan xStorage,* and *Enphase Encharge.*

The *Tesla Solar Plus Storage* system integrates solar panels (or roof tiles) with the power cell battery. The system is designed to power your home, automobile, and other household devices from solar energy.

Solar Energy

Solar radiation is light emitted from the sun. Solar energy is also known as electromagnetic radiation. While every location on Earth receives some sunlight over a year, the amount of solar radiation that reaches any one spot on Earth's surface varies. Solar technologies are designed to capture this radiation and turn it into useful forms of energy.

"Photovoltaic" (PV) technology consists of materials and devices that convert sunlight into electrical energy. A single PV device is known as a "cell." Each small cell typically produces about 1 or 2 watts of power. To boost the power output of PV cells, they are connected together in chains to form larger units, known as modules or "panels."

The infographic below breaks out the various components required for a solar energy system for a residential home. The "inverter" is a powered electronic device that converts electricity generated by the solar panels from Direct Current (DC) to Alternating Current (AC). AC electricity is used to power appliances in the home. The "charge controller" is an electronic power device that manages energy storage in batteries.[91]

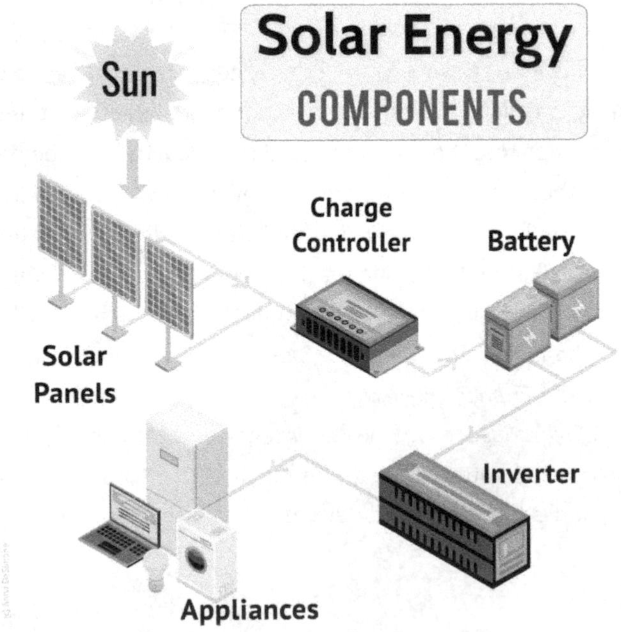

Solar panels can be used individually or connected to form "arrays." One or more of the arrays are connected to the "electrical grid" from a utility company to complete the PV system.[92] Solar systems include mounting structures that point the panels toward the sun. Some systems include a rotating solar tracker that allows the system to produce more energy by following the sun. Solar energy can also be used to heat a building's hot water. *(See Chapter 2, Heating, Ventilation, and Air Conditioning, Solar Hot Water Heating.)*

> **The price of solar electricity has dropped 89% in the past 10 years.**[93]
>
> —Energy Central

As previously stated, the average household uses 909-kilowatt hours (kWh) of energy each month, which is approximately 10,000 kWh annually. According to Energy Sage, a 10-kilowatt solar energy system will cover 100% of electrical needs of a household with an annual energy use of 10,000 kWh.[94]

Solar Reviews reports, "As the cost of solar continues to get cheaper, more people are choosing to install larger solar system sizes, and 10-kW solar systems are becoming an increasingly popular alternative energy solution for large homes and small offices."[95]

The number of solar panels required to power a 10-kW system ranges from 30 to 40 solar panels, depending upon the watt size of the panel. For example, a 300-watt panel requires 34 panels, versus 28 panels for a 350-watt panel, according to Solar Reviews.

Ideally, at least 600 square feet of south-facing roof space is required, however solar energy has shown success in homes with east- or west-facing roofs. Panels can be placed on any type of roof, and specialized mounting equipment can be used for tile roofs. Panels can be placed on garages or in the ground using brackets.

The latest trend is a "solar carport," which is a structure consisting of a solar-paneled roof that is supported by posts. It's designed for parking your car, and to also charge your electric automobiles, e-bikes, or garden tools.

> **Solar is becoming a large part of the Canadian Energy Solution. Across Canada, many homes meet 20% to 50% of their annual power needs from their rooftop system.[96]**
>
> —HES PV, Ltd.

Natural Resources Canada reports that Canada's use of solar energy has increased in recent years, and the potential is higher in the central regions. Many Canadian cities have solar potential that is comparable internationally to many major cities, and about half of Canada's residential electricity requirements could be met by installing solar panels on the roofs of residential buildings.[97]

The Canadian Ministry of Natural Resources has launched a web-mapping tool that calculates the solar potential of any location in Canada. The application allows users to view sun-tracking data, solar PV potential, and daily global isolation rates from a dataset of 3,500 municipalities.[98]

U.S. Resources:

Department of Energy
https://www.energy.gov/eere/solar/solar-energy-resources

Energy Sage
https://www.energysage.com

Solar Reviews
https://www.solarreviews.com

Canada Resources:

HES PV Canada
https://hespv.ca/residential-solar-energy-systems

Solar Energy Society of Canada
https://solarenergycanada.org/solar-energy-calculator/

Solar Photovoltaic Web-mapping Tool
https://fgp-pgf.maps.arcgis.com/apps/webappviewer/

Geothermal Energy

Geothermal energy comes from layers far beneath Earth. Thermal properties within the core are collected by a ground-level heat pump to heat and cool the home. Geothermal energy is clean—and considered to be the most eco-friendly solution because an entire home can be heated and cooled without the use of fossil fuels such as coal, gas, or oil.

Geothermal energy is available 24 hours a day, 365 days a year, and with a nearly unlimited supply. Power plants have average availabilities of 90% or higher, compared to about 75% for coal plants. Geothermal power is home-grown, reducing dependence on foreign oil.[99]

Hot and cold properties collected from Earth's core are fed through a "geothermal heat pump," sometimes referred to as a geo-exchange. The heat pump is able to heat and cool the home and, if equipped, can also supply the house with hot water. Unlike ground-source heat pump systems, which utilize shallow horizontal fields to store and retrieve energy, geothermal energy is extracted from a deep well.

"Hydrothermal resources" are reservoirs of hot water that exist at varying temperatures and depths below Earth's surface. Deep wells of a mile or more are drilled into underground reservoirs to tap steam and very hot water that can be brought to the surface to generate electricity.[100]

According to the Center for Sustainable Systems at the University of Michigan, the United States continues to generate the most geothermal electricity in the world, mostly in western states.[101]

The Energy Information Administration reports that California has the highest share of geothermal energy, followed by Nevada. Other states with geothermal power plants include Utah, Oregon, Hawaii, Idaho, and New Mexico.[102]

Dandelion Energy is actively installing geothermal heating and cooling systems in New York and other areas in the northeast. Dandelion's system was originally conceived at X, Alphabet's innovation lab.[103]

Geothermal technology can reduce energy consumption by as much as 65%.[104]

—U.S. Department of Energy

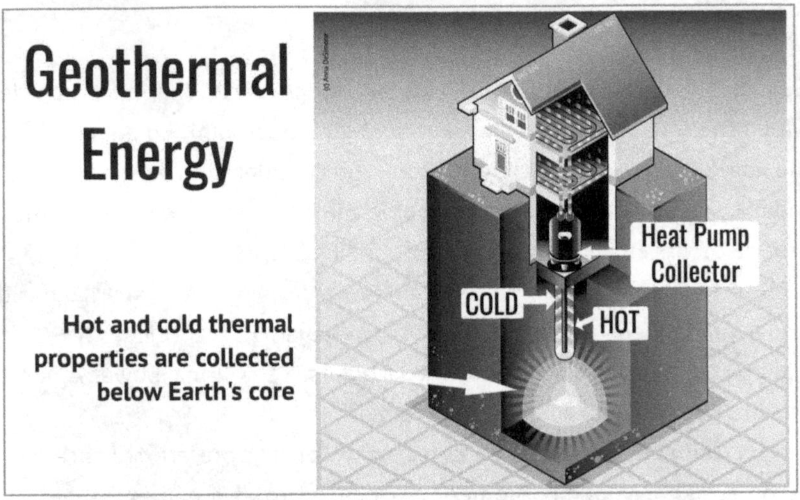

The infographic describes a "vertical loop" system, involving two 4-inch thick pipes drilled at least 100 feet deep into the ground; and systems can require depths of up to 300 feet. The pipes form a U-bend at the bottom to form a loop.

Hot and cold thermal properties are collected through separate chambers of piping and fed through a heat pump collector. The energy is used to heat the home in the winter and cool the home in the summer. Optional equipment can be added to heat hot water.

A "horizontal loop" geothermal system involves the same type of collectors and heat pump; however, pipes are buried about 6 to 10 feet deep and spread out over a broader area of ground.

According to Natural Resources Canada, many parts of Canada are home to the natural conditions required for the extraction of geothermal energy, specifically in parts of Western Canada. The highest temperature geothermal resources are located in British Columbia, Northwest Territories, Yukon, and Alberta. Heat and power generation projects are being considered with the demonstration projects under way. The South Meager Geothermal project in British Columbia is the most advanced geothermal power project in Canada.[105]

To find out where geothermal energy is available, you can view maps that are regularly updated by the U.S. Department of Energy (DOE) and the Canadian Geothermal Energy Association (CanGEA).

View updated geothermal maps in the U.S.
https://www.energy.gov/eere/geothermal/geothermal-maps

View updated geothermal maps in Canada
https://www.cangea.ca/project-map.html

Wind Energy

The United States and Canada are listed in the top eight wind-producing countries in the world.[106] The terms "wind energy" and "wind power" both describe the process by which the wind is used to generate mechanical power or electricity. A generator is used to convert this mechanical power into electricity. On its own, the mechanical power can be used for a specific task such as grinding grain or pumping water.

Wind is a form of solar energy caused by a combination of three concurrent events: a) the sun unevenly heating the atmosphere, b) the irregularities of Earth's surface, and c) the rotation of Earth.[107]

"Wind turbines" turn wind energy into electricity using the aerodynamic force from the rotor blades, which work like an airplane wing or helicopter rotor blade. When wind flows across the blade, the air pressure on one side of the blade decreases. The difference in air pressure across the two sides of the blade creates both lift and drag. The force of the lift is stronger than the drag and this causes the rotor to spin. This aerodynamic force enables the generator to create electricity.

Most wind turbines fall into two basic types, the "vertical axis" and the "horizontal axis." Both types are illustrated below.

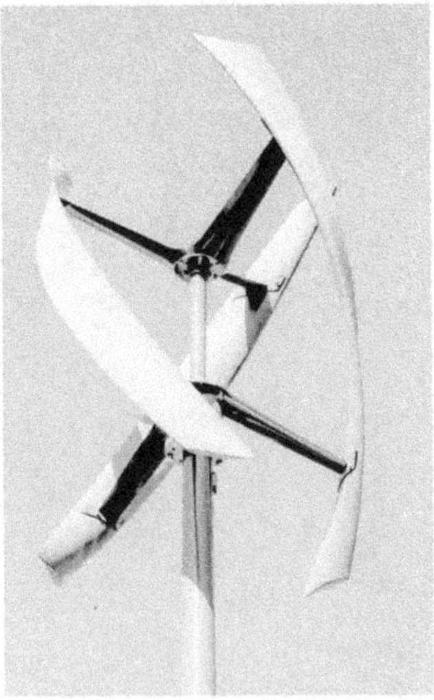

Shutterstock Images

Vertical Axis Wind Turbine

Turbines are omni-directional and do not need to be adjusted to point to the wind.

The Darrieus model is commonly known as the "eggbeater."

Shutterstock Images

Horizontal Axis Wind Turbine

Turbines generally have three blades and operate upwind.

The turbine pivots at the top of the tower so that the blades face into the wind.

Small and Community Wind Turbines

Small and community wind turbines are suitable for private residential homes and are designed to offset all (or a portion of) energy consumption. Systems are also called "distributed wind," and utilize a small wind turbine mounted on a tower. The higher the tower, the more power the wind system can produce.

Most small wind turbines manufactured today are horizontal-axis, upwind machines with two or three blades that may be made of fiberglass or composite materials. Most turbine manufacturers provide wind energy system packages that include towers, along with a range of other equipment such as batteries, controller, grounding system, and foundation for the tower.[108]

The Department of Energy administers a website called WINDExchange that offers comprehensive guidance and services. From the site you can research turbine models, estimate costs, find an installer, and apply for a permit.

Department of Energy WINDExchange
https://windexchange.energy.gov/small-community-wind-handbook

Canada Wind Energy

Canada's geography makes it ideally suited to capitalize on large amounts of wind energy. The benefits of increased deployment of wind energy include grid-wide energy savings and reductions in greenhouse gas emissions and air contaminants.

In Canada, wind energy has attracted $23 billion in investments. There are 301 wind farms operating coast to coast and 6,771 wind turbines. Canada finished 2019 with installed wind energy capacity to power approximately 3.4 million homes.[109]

> Canada has outlined a future strategy for wind energy that would reach a capacity of 55 gigawatts by 2025, meeting 20% of Canada's energy needs.[110]
>
> —Canadian Wind Energy Association (CanWEA)

To use wind energy at your home, a "small-scale wind turbine" can be connected to the electricity grid through your power provider, or it can stand alone (off-grid). This makes wind energy an option for remote communities that are not connected to the provincial or territorial grid. Several provinces have programs for individuals and businesses that want to generate wind energy using small-scale or microgeneration wind turbines.[111]

Resources:

Canadian Wind Energy Association—Small-Scale Wind Energy
Includes searchable links for each province
www.canwea.ca/wind-energy/small-wind-energy/

Distributed Wind Energy Association (U.S. and Canada)
https://distributedwind.org/links-resources/

Hydro-electric Power

When flowing water is harnessed and used to create electricity, it is called "hydropower" or "hydro-electric power." Because the water cycle is an endless, constantly recharging system, hydropower is considered a renewable energy.

Micro-hydropower

"Micro-hydropower" is a form of hydropower available to homeowners who have flowing water located on their property. Micro-hydropower systems can generate up to 100 kilowatts of electricity, however a 10-kilowatt system generally can provide enough power for a large home.

A sufficient quantity of falling water must be available, which generally means that hilly or mountainous sites are best. Other considerations include power output, economics, permits, and water rights. A micro-hydropower system needs a turbine, pump, or waterwheel to transform the energy of flowing water into rotational energy, which is converted into electricity. Commercially available turbines and generators are usually sold as a package, and components will depend upon whether the system is stand alone or grid connected.

Installation of a micro-hydropower system on residential property requires a permit and validation of water rights. Procedures vary depending upon whether the system is stand alone or grid connected. You will also need to follow requirements to ensure that your micro-hydropower system will have minimal impact on the environment. The permit process is relatively straightforward if you are not planning to sell power to a utility.

To assess whether or not a micro-hydropower system would be feasible on your property, you need to determine the amount of power that can potentially be obtained from the flowing water. The assessment involves two basic factors, "head" and "flow."

The vertical distance that water can fall is called the head, and the quantity of water falling is called the flow. There are relatively simple mathematical steps that determine the system's output, measured in "watts."[112]

The U.S. Department of Energy publishes a comprehensive guide called *Planning a Micro-Hydropower System,* which includes detailed steps and instructions for planning and operating a micro-hydropower system.

Natural Resources Canada publishes a comprehensive guide called *Introduction to Micro-Hydropower Systems* that includes detailed instructions for planning and operating a micro-hydropower system.

Resources:

U.S. Department of Energy, Planning a Micro-Hydropower System
https://www.energy.gov/energysaver/planning-microhydropower-system

Canada Natural Resources, Introduction to Micro-Hydropower Systems
https://www.nrcan.gc.ca/sites/www.nrcan.gc.ca/files/canmetenergy/files/pubs/Intro_MicroHydro_ENG.pdf

Energy Systems and Design, Waterford, New Brunswick
International supplier of micro-hydropower products
https://microhydropower.com

International Information Portal
http://www.microhydropower.net

Biomass

Biomass is an organic renewable energy source that includes materials such as agriculture and forest residues, energy crops, and algae. Biomass is a modern name for the ancient technology of burning plant or animal material for production of electricity or heat. In many developing countries, biomass is currently the only source of fuel for domestic use.

Biomass resources used either directly as a fuel or converted to another form or energy product are commonly referred to as "feedstocks." Biomass feedstocks include dedicated energy crops, agricultural crop residues, forestry residues, algae, wood processing residues, municipal waste, and wet waste.[113]

Forest feedstocks include residues left after logging timber or whole-tree biomass harvested explicitly for biomass. Woody debris is collected for use in bioenergy, and harvesting excessive woody biomass can reduce the risk of fire as well as aid in forest restoration.

Wood processing yields byproducts and waste streams that are collectively called wood processing residues. The processing of wood for products or pulp produces unused sawdust, bark, branches, leaves, and needles. These residues are relatively inexpensive sources of biomass that can be converted into biofuels or bioproducts.

According to the U.S. Department of Energy, agricultural and forestry waste such as corn stover (the remaining husks, stalks, stems, and leaves of corn) and lawn clippings can be used as a source of sustainable fuel to power vehicles of all types. These sources of non-food biomass contain the raw materials and molecular compounds needed to create cellulosic ethanol, a fuel source that has the potential to slash carbon emissions by more than 80% when replacing gasoline.

Local farmers have an opportunity to generate additional income by harvesting corn stover and selling it to a cellulosic biorefinery. The corn stover is stored at the biorefinery until it is ready to be processed into cellulosic ethanol.[114]

Canada has a large supply of renewable forest biomass, as well as access to forest industry by-products and residues. British Columbia, Ontario, Alberta, Quebec, and New Brunswick are the provinces with the largest biomass capacity and generation. Bioenergy accounts for approximately 6% of Canada's total energy supply. Scientists and engineers at CanmetENERGY are at the forefront of innovative technology developments. The Canadian Biomass Innovation Network (CBIN) supports the development of a sustainable Canadian bioeconomy.[115]

Biofuel

When biomass is processed into a fuel to produce heat or power, it is called "biofuel." Biofuels can be produced from plants or from agricultural waste. Industrial wastes that have a biological origin can also be used as biofuel.

Renewable biofuels generally involve contemporary carbon fixation, such as those that occur in plants or microalgae through the process of photosynthesis. If the biomass used in the production of biofuel can regrow quickly, the fuel is generally considered to be a form of renewable energy.

One of the top choices for energy alternatives is bioheat made from wood heating technology. "Bioheat" is the heat produced when biofuel is combusted. Modern bioheat systems are ideal for providing space heat and domestic hot water for private homes. Types of solid wood biofuel include cordwood, wood chips, wood briquettes, and wood pellets.[116]

Combustion systems that can be used include cordwood stoves, pellet stoves, cordwood furnaces, pellet furnaces, cordwood boilers, pellet boilers, and wood chip boilers. Furnace models can accommodate a fan and duct system to move hot air throughout the home and are controlled using a central thermostat.

According to the Ontario-based Centre for Research & Innovation in the Bio-Economy, bioheating technology is widely used in Europe, Alaska, the northeastern United States, and across Canada.[117]

CHAPTER 4

Net Zero and Energy-Rated Homes

WHAT IS A NET ZERO HOME? When a home produces its own energy from a renewable source such as solar or wind, and over the course of 12 months the system generates the same amount of energy used by your home, the effect is known as "net zero."

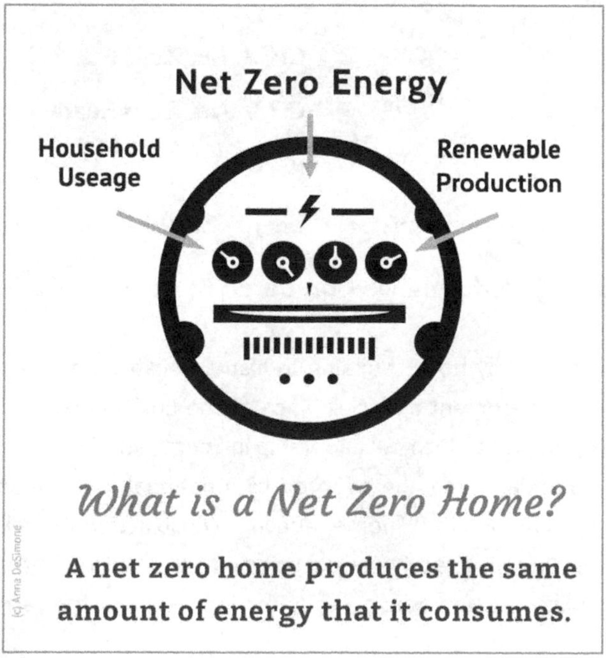

Net Zero Energy
Household Useage
Renewable Production
What is a Net Zero Home?
A net zero home produces the same amount of energy that it consumes.
(c) Anna DeSimone

Net Zero Homes

Commonly referred to as "zero energy homes," a net zero home produces 100% of its electricity from renewable energy. As explained earlier in Chapter 3, renewable energy systems operate under a two-way connection with the local utility grid. When energy produced by the system becomes insufficient, electrical power begins to draw from the grid. The net zero calculation is based on grid-supplied vs. site-generated electricity measured over the course of 12 months.

Net zero homes are basically high-performance homes. They are built "above-code," which means construction standards extend beyond the legal requirements. Above-code homes are well-insulated and built with other features that increase energy performance.

As more robust features and technologies are added, performance levels increase incrementally. When a renewable energy component is installed, performance levels reach the top of the spectrum. The chart below from the Canadian Home Builders' Association (CHBA) illustrates the approximate energy performance levels of four voluntary programs in Canada:[118]

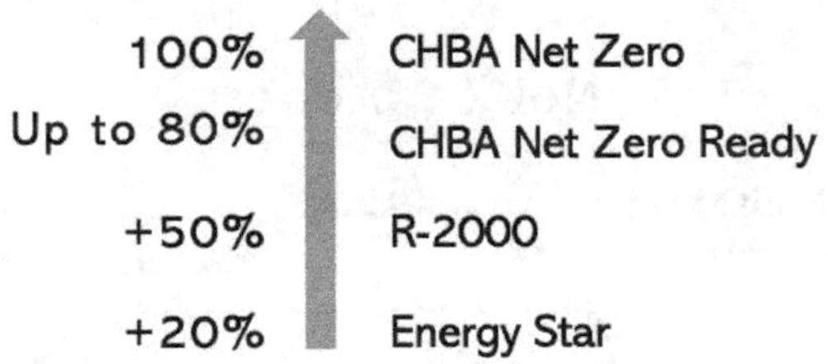

Energy Performance Compared to Building Code

In the eco-friendly home building industry, construction standards are developed by government agencies, such as the Environmental Protection Agency, or by institutes such as Leadership in Energy and Environmental Design (LEED). Standards may be adopted by a national building society and incorporated as a voluntary "home labeling" construction model. On a nationwide level, builders receive education and support from industry trade groups, enabling greater transparency for homebuyers for various home models.

After construction is completed, a third-party "energy rater" independently tests the homes. Methodologies may include the Home Energy Rating System (known as HERS), Canada's EnerGuide Rating System, and others. The foremost building certifications and energy rating programs are explained in Chapter 5, *Energy Scores and Building Certifications.*

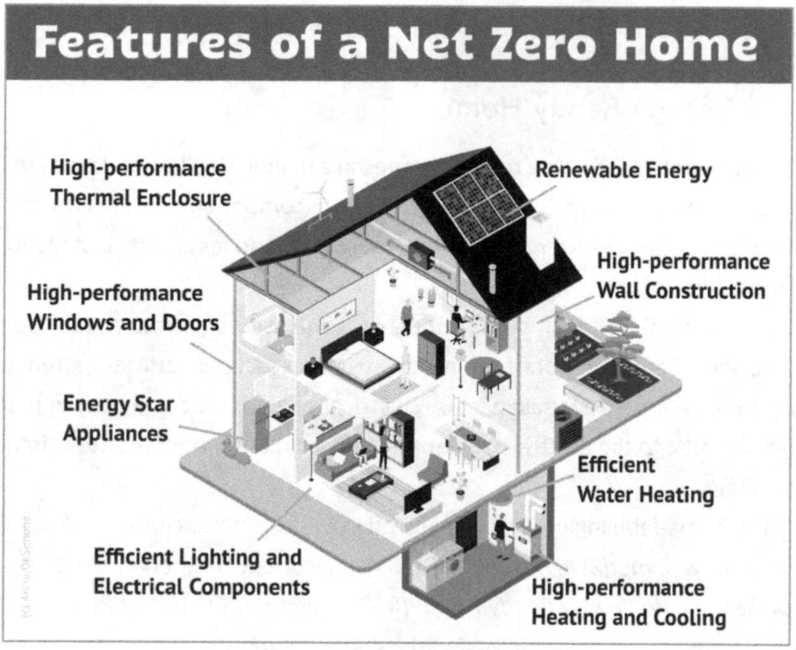

The infographic lists the fundamental elements of a high-performance home—plus the renewable energy component. Each feature illustrated is explained in Chapter 2, *Whole House Efficiency Blueprint.*

Although each element will function individually, as a whole they operate on an interdependent level. Even the best heating and cooling system won't reach its fullest potential if the home is not sufficiently insulated.

It is important to consider energy efficiency on a whole-house level when selecting options on a new home purchase or planning a renovation project. For example, if your retrofit plans include a heating and cooling upgrade, keeping older—but operable—components will save a little money upfront. However, an outdated component can become the "weakest link" within the HVAC system, impeding energy performance, and may cost more to replace later on.

Just about any home has the potential to be net zero—even homes that are 100 years old. Frequently called a "deep retrofit," homes undergo a series of efficiency measures, along with installation or upgrading of appliances. Decisions about features and options must be affordable and practical. It may be more cost-effective to install all of the energy-efficient features up front—and install the renewable energy system at a later date. This practical solution is our next topic, "zero energy ready" homes.

Zero Energy Ready Homes

Also known as "renewable ready," homes are built with all the features of a net zero home—minus the renewable energy component. Homes are prewired for renewable energy, enabling a seamless and less costly installation in the future.

Homes that are "solar ready" undergo a site assessment to ensure adequate solar potential. Roof framing construction assures sufficient strength to support the photovoltaic panels. Electrical wiring includes a built-in path from the attic to the electric panel that has "solar components-ready" circuit breakers.

The home-labeling programs featured in this chapter include *the Zero Energy Ready Home (ZERH)* from the U.S. Department of Energy, the *Energy Star Renewable Energy Ready Home (RERH)*, and the CHBA *Net Zero Ready* home from the Canadian Home Builders' Association.

Zero Energy Terminology

A number of terms and definitions on the topic of zero energy are used interchangeably, and some are more narrowly defined. As an example, when a renewable energy system produces 100% of electricity to power the home, and other fuels (such as natural gas) are used for heating, the effect might be defined as "net zero electricity."

It is important to keep in mind that many definitions are broad, and also apply to industrial buildings and multi-family apartment buildings. Generally, metrics for such projects encompass carbon emissions factors and a building's impact on the environment. Terminology that is commonly associated with zero energy, such as zero carbon, are explained further below.

Green Construction

The term "eco-friendly" construction universally applies to energy-efficient homes as well as "green-built" homes. According to the World Green Building Council, "A green building is a building that, in its design, construction or operation, reduces or eliminates negative impacts, and can create positive impacts on our climate and natural environment."[119]

Today's building standards, including each of the programs featured in this book, are built in accordance with green-building protocols. The energy-efficiency standards of a home, however, are an added dimension.

Chapter 5, *Energy Scores and Building Certifications*, includes information about industry trade groups such as the Canada Green Building Council, and national certifications such as the National Green Building Standard (NGBS) in the U.S.

Zero Carbon Homes

A different set of metrics applies to the term "zero carbon." In the building industry, the measurement of carbon emissions extends back to the manufacturing facility of construction materials. For that reason, prefabricated or factory-built homes may be described as "zero carbon." Zero carbon metrics may also take into account the occupant's transportation usage. Renewable offsets purchased by a homeowner can effectively render the household's footprint as "carbon neutral."

"Embodied carbon" is the carbon and other greenhouse gas emissions that are part of the materials, equipment, processes, and contents of a building. "Operational carbon" refers to the greenhouse gases released by the energy used in a building for heating, cooling, ventilation, lighting, equipment, and appliances. "Maintenance carbon" is the carbon or carbon equivalent released by operations and products needed for maintaining the building, including repair, replacement, and remodeling.[120]

According to the nonprofit environmental educational organization, Zero Energy Project, "Zero carbon is a commonly used term that refers to eliminating all greenhouse gases (GHGs) involved in a project. It encompasses all climate-related emissions, including carbon-dioxide, methane, ozone, black carbon, and fluorocarbon compounds. For simplicity, the terms zero carbon

(CO_2) or zero carbon equivalents (CO_2e) are used to include all these greenhouse gases. A home or building with zero greenhouse gas emissions, whether from carbon dioxide or other greenhouse gases, has zero global warming potential."[121]

Cradle-to-Grave Carbon Footprint

The "cradle-to-grave" concept is based on a lifecycle analysis that extends beyond energy performance. According to the Canadian environmental design company, ECOHome, "The lifecycle analysis of a building assesses the potential environmental impact of a building from start to finish. In the interest of completeness, factors considered are as follows: human health, the quality of ecosystems, climate change, and use of resources."[122]

> **A zero net energy home or building focuses on operational energy, whereas a zero carbon building offsets its yearly carbon emissions from operations plus its embodied carbon emissions.**
>
> —ECOHome, Canada

ECOHome further explains, "For its part, the carbon footprint focuses only on the greenhouse gases (GHGs) involved in the life of a building. About half of a building's carbon footprint comes from 'embodied carbon,' also known as 'grey energy.'

The other half comes from 'operating energy.' The grey energy consumed during the construction phase causes a one-off embodied carbon emission. When the building is completed, this carbon footprint quantity no longer rises.

On the other hand, the operation of the building emits carbon throughout the life span of the building through energy utilization for heating, air conditioning, lighting, and appliances. Both grey energy and operating energy release carbon dioxide into the atmosphere—the main difference is when they are produced."[123]

Positive Energy Homes

Imagine your utility meter working in reverse. Energy that is produced above and beyond your home's electrical needs is known as "positive energy." This effect is often described as "carbon positive," and would likely be noted as "excess generation" on your monthly utility bill.

A net zero home can be upgraded by installing an "oversize" system, thus producing even more electricity. For example, components such as micro-inverters can be installed to accommodate the addition of more solar panels to an existing system. Excess generation from a positive energy home can be sold to the utility grid or converted to billing credits. There are cash rewards for positive energy. If permissible under your utility agreement, you can sell renewable energy certificates (RECs) or solar renewable energy certificates (SRECs), as explained in Chapter 3, *Renewable Energy*.

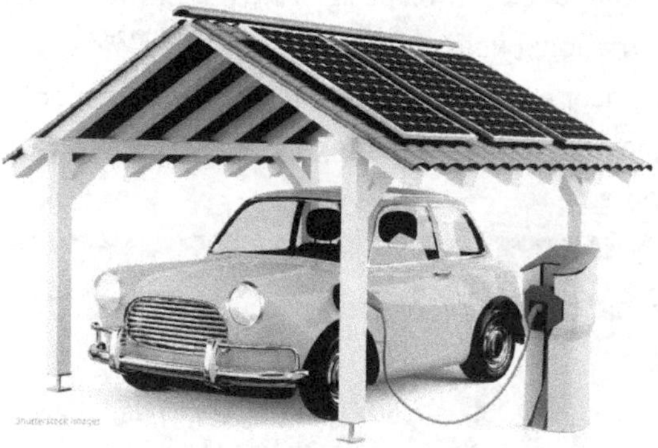

Solar energy carports can power your car, e-bike, and garden tools.

The number of solar photovoltaic panels required for electric car chargers is based on the vehicle's battery storage capacity and your projected automobile mileage. If your solar panels are producing just enough energy to power your home appliances, you might need anywhere from 6 to 12 additional solar panels to power a car. There are components available, such as the *SolarEdge* EV charging inverter, which pairs a charger and a DC inverter into one device.

According to Zero Energy Project, "The energy produced by each 1 kW solar PV system in the northern part of the U.S. can power an electric car, such as the *Nissan Leaf*, for an average of 12 miles a day, or 70 to 80 miles per charge."[124]

Passive House

One of the most renowned principles associated with energy-efficient homes is the "passive house." Simply put, a passive home makes use of whatever is free—which is always a good place to start. According to the Passive House Institute, "A passive house is a tried-and-true construction concept that can be applied to any building. A passive home makes efficient use of the sun, and strategies involve the use of heat recovery systems and other internal heat sources."

Even in the coldest of winters, conventional heating systems are often unnecessary. During warmer weather, a passive home makes use of cooling techniques such as strategic shading to keep the house cool. Special windows and a highly insulated building keep desired warmth in the house—or undesirable heat out.[125]

"Doing more with less" is the fundamental design concept of the passive house, according to the International Passive House Association.[126] Several of the home labeling and certification programs described in this chapter incorporate principles of the passive house. The infographic below highlights the primary construction elements.

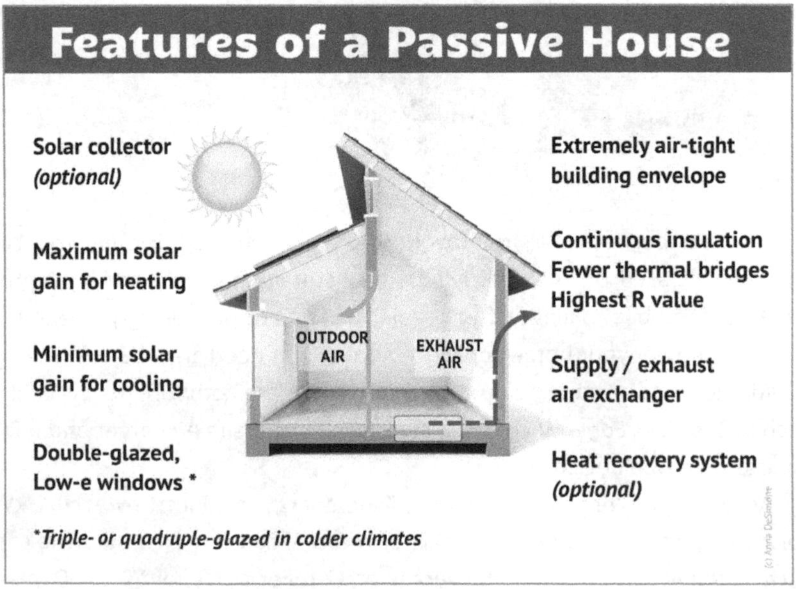

Home Labeling Programs

The remainder of this chapter features a number of new home construction programs that are administered by national building societies and available from builders on a nationwide level.

In the United States, the National Association of Home Builders (NAHB) supports the voluntary use of energy labels and other efforts to encourage the disclosure of energy information to homeowners and home buyers. Uniform labeling guidelines that take into account established energy codes, address liability issues, recognize the greater energy efficiency of newly constructed homes and integrate with and complement nationally accepted rating certifications, such as the Home Innovation National Green Building Standard (NGBS) Green Certification Program.[127]

In Canada, the Canadian Home Builders Association launched its Net Zero program, continuing CHBA's long history in leading energy efficiency in residential construction. The program provides the industry and consumers with a clearly defined and rigorous two-tiered technical requirement that recognizes Net Zero and Net Zero Ready Homes, and identifies the builders and renovators who provide them.[128]

> **Residential energy labeling programs produce an assessment of a home's energy performance and compares it to that of other similar homes. They provide valuable information for homeowners, homebuyers, and other stakeholders such as real estate professionals, appraisers, lenders, and contractors.**
>
> —National Association of State Energy Officials[129]

Certain labeling programs, such as the *Zero Energy Ready Home*, have a "pre-requisite baseline" construction rule, where standards must be equivalent to another labeling program, such as *Energy Star Certified Homes*. In addition, the United States and Canada mutually recognize building standards such as the International Energy Conservation Code (IECC). For that reason, program descriptions are presented in a progressive order according to level of performance—starting with energy-efficient homes and concluding with Net Zero homes.

Energy Star Certified Homes

Homes that are eligible to earn the Energy Star label include single-family, multifamily, and manufactured housing. As of 2020, more than 2 million Energy Star certified homes and apartments have been built. New homes that have been built under the *Energy Star New Homes Program* have shown to be 10% more energy efficient than homes built to code and achieve a 20% improvement on average.[130] Features and benefits include:

- High-efficiency heating and cooling
- Complete thermal enclosure system
- Efficient lighting and appliances
- Water protection system
- Independent inspections and testing

In order for a home to be certified, the home must be built in accordance with required standards for the building envelope, insulation, windows, doors, heating, cooling, water heater, ductwork, lighting, and appliances. The home must be inspected by a qualified energy rater.

Canada Energy Star Certified Homes

Natural Resources Canada oversees the certified homes program in Canada. Construction requirements align with the above-described U.S. requirements. Homes are evaluated, inspected and labeled by a third-party energy advisor.[131] Features and benefits include the following:

- Efficient heating and cooling systems
- Additional air-sealing
- High performance windows, doors, and skylights
- Whole house ventilation system
- Energy Star certified products

U.S. Resources:

Energy Star Fact Sheets by State

https://www.energystar.gov/about/state_fact_sheets

Find a Builder

https://www.energystar.gov/index.cfm?fuseaction=new_homes_partners.locator&s_code=AL

Find a Home Rater

https://www.energystar.gov/homes_tr_audience/raters

Canada Resources:

Energy Star Certified Home Information

https://www.nrcan.gc.ca/energy-efficiency/energy-star-canada/about-energy-star-canada/energy-star-announcements/energy-starr-certified-homes/5057

Find a Builder or Service Provider

https://www2.nrcan.gc.ca/oee/nh-mn/f-t/index.cfm?fuseaction=s.ssf&language=eng

Guide to Energy Star Certified Homes and Label

https://www.nrcan.gc.ca/energy-efficiency/energy-star-canada/energy-star-new-homes/guide-energy-star-certified-homes/12348

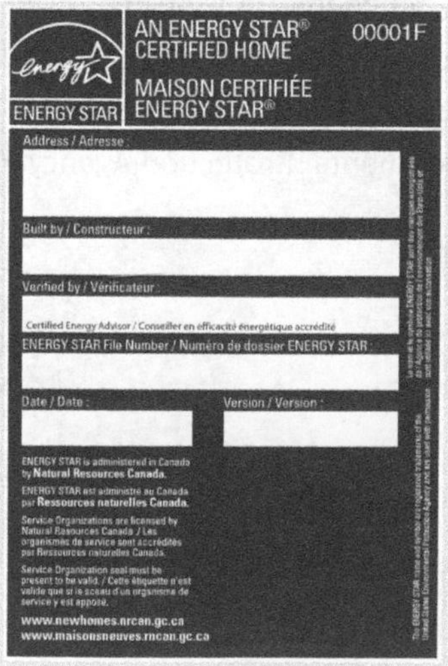

Home Innovation
NGBS GREEN CERTIFIED™

National Green Building Standard

In the United States, the ICC 700 National Green Building Standard™ (NGBS) is the only green building rating system created exclusively for homes and multifamily buildings that has been approved by ANSI, the American National Standards Institute, as an American National Standard. The NGBS provides practices for the design, construction, and certification of new single-family homes and renovations.

Under the NGBS, single-family homes have two compliance choices. For a home to attain any certification level, all applicable mandatory provisions must be correctly implemented. Homes can earn the Certified level if they comply with all applicable green practices requiring homes to be designed and constructed to be more efficient than current code-compliant homes, and to include building practices that ensure the home provides for a healthier indoor environment, is more water efficient, and is more durable. Alternatively, homes can earn Bronze, Silver, Gold, or Emerald certification.[132]

Home Innovation Research Labs is a wholly owned, independent subsidiary of the National Association of Home Builders (NAHB) and serves as Adopting Entity of the National Green Building Standard, providing certification services to builders, developers, and remodelers nationwide for the NGBS Green certification program. The certification process can also include water efficiency in accordance with the Environmental Protection Agency's WaterSense program.

NGBS Green Home Information
https://www.ngbs.com

Single-family Green Certification
https://www.homeinnovation.com/-/media/Files/Certification/Green_Building/Single-Family_NGBS_Green_Brochure.pdf

Natural Resources Canada

R-2000

R-2000 is a voluntary standard administered by Natural Resources Canada and is delivered through a network of service organizations and professionals across Canada. Houses built to the R-2000 standard typically exceed the energy performance requirements of the current Canadian building codes and are recognized to meet a high standard of environmental responsibility. The R-2000 program is the result of 25 years of intensive research and development by the government of Canada and its industry partners.[133] The features of the program include the following:

- Environmentally responsible materials
- 30% more energy efficient than conventional new home
- Minimum *EnerGuide* efficiency rating of 80
- Clean air features and improved indoor air quality
- Consistent temperatures with year-round comfort
- Fewer moisture problems
- Certification process and independent inspection

Information about R-2000

www.newhomes.nrcan.gc.ca

Find a new energy-efficient home in Canada

https://www.nrcan.gc.ca/energy-efficiency/energy-efficiency-homes/buying-energy-efficient-new-home/20556

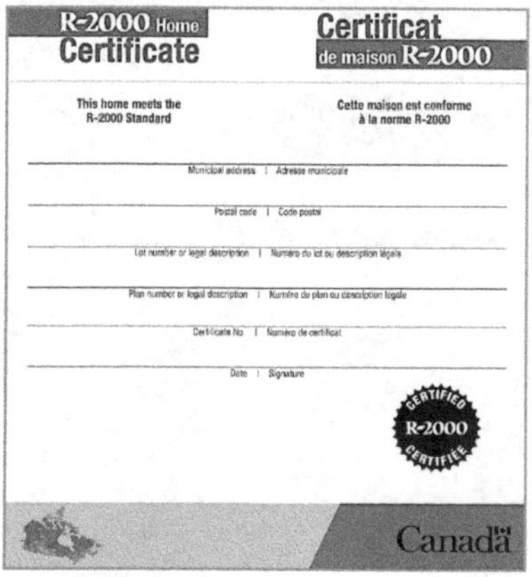
R-2000 Home Certificate

Certificat de maison R-2000

This home meets the R-2000 Standard

Cette maison est conforme à la norme R-2000

Municipal address | Adresse municipale

Postal code | Code postal

Lot number or legal description | Numéro du lot ou description légale

Plan number or legal description | Numéro du plan ou description légale

Certificate No | Numéro de certificat

Date | Signature

CERTIFIED R-2000 CERTIFIÉE

Canadä

U.S. Department of Energy Zero Energy Ready Home

The U.S. Department of Energy administers a certification program called "Zero Energy Ready Home" (ZERH). In order for the home to receive the ZERH certificate, construction must comply with a strict set of energy-efficient standards, including any state-specific environmental codes. Builders must employ qualified and credentialed HVAC contractors.

Mandatory requirements include a baseline Energy Star certified home; a building envelope meeting Energy Star requirements for ceiling, wall, floor, and slab insulation; optimum HVAC air handling and duct systems; water efficiency and hot water delivery systems; Energy Star refrigerators, dishwashers, and clothes washers; 80% of lighting fixtures or lamps that are Energy Star qualified; Energy Star ventilation and ceiling fans; and air quality that is certified under Environmental Protection Agency standards. Provisions must be in place for future installation of solar photovoltaic (PV) renewable energy.[134]

The ZERH program builds upon the requirements and infrastructure from complementary federal government new home labeling programs, such as the Energy Star Certification, explained earlier. ZERH certification entails a home energy assessment and DOE *Home Energy Score.*

Zero Ready Complete List of Requirements
www.energy.gov/eere/buildings/zero-energy-ready-homes

DOE Zero Energy Ready Home Partner Locator
https://www5.eere.energy.gov/buildings/residential/locator

Energy Star
Renewable Energy Ready Home

The Environmental Protection Agency (EPA) developed the specifications for the Energy Star Renewable Energy Ready Home (RERH). The EPA aims to educate builders on how to assess and equip new homes with a set of features that makes it easier and less expensive for homeowners to install solar energy systems after the home is constructed.

The RERH specification and checklist takes a builder and a project design team through the necessary steps of assessing the home's solar resource potential and outfitting a home with the necessary minimum structural and system components needed to support a complete renewable energy system.[135]

The EPA provides a "solar site assessment tool" to help homebuyers determine whether or not a proposed solar array location offers sufficient solar resources to support the operation of a future energy system. Meeting the recommended elements of the RERH specification may not be possible in all home building situations due to factors such as excessive shading on the proposed array location. The program's main website provides numerous checklists and helpful information. Key web resources are provided below.

RERH Program
https://www.energystar.gov/partner_resources/residential_new/related_programs/rerh

RERH Solar Photovoltaic Specifications
https://www.energystar.gov/sites/default/files/asset/document/Renewable_Energy_PV.pdf

RERH Solar Site Assessment Tool
https://www.energystar.gov/partner_resources/residential_new/rerh/rerh_solar_site_assessment_tool

Canadian Home Builders' Association

- CHBA Net Zero
- CHBA Net Zero Ready
- CHBA Net Zero Renovation

The Canadian Home Builders' Association (CHBA) supports a full spectrum of voluntary energy performance levels to provide Canadians with higher performing homes. The CHBA Net Zero Home Labelling Program has been designed so that a home could still qualify for Net Zero Ready, R-2000, or Energy Star, if Net Zero isn't achievable.

A national network of CHBA Net Zero Qualified Service Organizations, Energy Advisors, and Trainers will work directly with the builders and renovators to design, model, test, and inspect each home.

Net Zero and Net Zero Ready Homes offer whole-house comfort, excellent indoor air quality, and superior energy performance using proven advanced technologies and construction practices. The result is a superior quality home that exceeds current and anticipated building code requirements. Each Net Zero and Net Zero Ready Home will be verified by government-licensed third-party Service Organizations and recognized by CHBA for its achievement.[136]

A Net Zero Home produces as much energy as it consumes and is up to 80% more energy efficient than a home built to conventional standards. Homes are built to higher standards than conventional new homes, and are more durable, with high-performance windows and better insulated walls and roof.

Advanced construction methods and materials, along with superior heating, cooling and ventilation equipment, provides even temperatures throughout the house and exceptional comfort all year round. Homes have excellent indoor air quality with a built-in filtered fresh air system and are equipped with water-saving fixtures and appliances.[137]

CHBA Net Zero Home

- Annual energy consumption is offset by onsite renewable energy generation
- Conforms to EnerGuide Rating System
- Air-tightness of >= 1.5 ACH@50 Pa
- Energy efficiency first approach: envelope is at least 33% more efficient than house built to code
- Program is fuel agnostic
- Highly efficient mechanical systems
- Energy monitor system tracks consumption and generation

CHBA Net Zero Ready Home

- Exact same home as above, except:
- Renewable energy generation of sufficient capacity is modelled but not yet installed
- Home is equipped for future solar

CHBA Net Zero Renovation

CHBA states, "Net Zero Homes are not just for new construction anymore." CHBA has developed tools and resources so that some homes could achieve a Net Zero label through deep energy retrofits. Some homes can more easily pursue a Net Zero Energy Renovation than others, and CHBA advises homeowners to meet with a qualified Net Zero renovator to determine the home's net zero energy potential.

CHBA Net Zero Programs
Find a Qualified Builder or Renovator
https://www.chba.ca/CHBA/BuyingNew/Net-Zero-Homes.aspx

zero
energy project

The Zero Energy Project is a non-profit educational organization whose goal is to help homebuyers, builders, designers, and real estate professionals take meaningful steps towards radically reducing carbon emissions and energy bills by building zero net energy homes and near zero energy homes.[138]
Zero Energy Project's key resources are provided below.

Find a Zero Energy Home Builder in U.S. or Canada
www.zeroenergyproject.org/zero-energy-home-builders/

Find a Zero Energy Home Development
https://zeroenergyproject.org/find/zero-energy-home-developments-multi-family-projects/

Find a Zero Energy Home Product
Search for air sealing systems, appliances, electric vehicle chargers, HVAC systems, heat pump water heaters, insulation, insulated wall assemblies, solar electric systems, storage batteries, ventilation systems, heat recovery systems, etc. used by builders in zero energy construction projects.
https://zeroenergyproject.org/zero-energy-home-products/

Find a Zero Energy Professional in the U.S. and Canada
Builders, designers, Energy Consultants, and Modular and Panelized Homes can be located using the flash map or search tools for any state or province.
https://zeroenergyproject.org/zero-energy-home-products/

Find an Energy Auditor or Consultant
https://zeroenergyproject.org/find/find-energy-auditors-zero-energy-retro-fitters/

Find a Green Realtor or Eco-friendly home
https://www.realtysagepros.com/?rid=zeroenergyproject

CHAPTER 5

Energy Scores and Building Certifications

ENERGY RATINGS & NEW HOME CERTIFICATIONS ADD VALUE. If you are exploring energy-efficient homes, you will notice there are dozens of building standards, certifications, and energy scores. Studies have shown that homes meeting certain environmental standards sell for a higher price, as explained in Chapter 9, *Financial Payback and True Cost of Home Ownership.*

In this chapter, you'll learn about the three foremost home energy rating systems in North America: the Department of Energy's Home Energy Score; EnerGuide from Canada Natural Resources; and HERS Energy Rating from the Residential Energy Services Network (RESNET).

Each of the three energy assessment programs follow substantially similar steps and procedures. For that reason, sample pages of an entire report are provided only for the U.S. Department of Energy program. Energy assessments are available to the public, and homeowners can order the same report that is used by builders.

This chapter also includes information about the councils and institutes that develop and implement sustainable and energy-efficient building certification programs.

Residential Energy Services Network (RESNET)

More than 3 million homes have been rated under a system that is known as the "Home Energy Rating System (HERS)." Illustrated below is a HERS Index Rating Chart, with infographics added by the author.[139]

Image source: RESNET

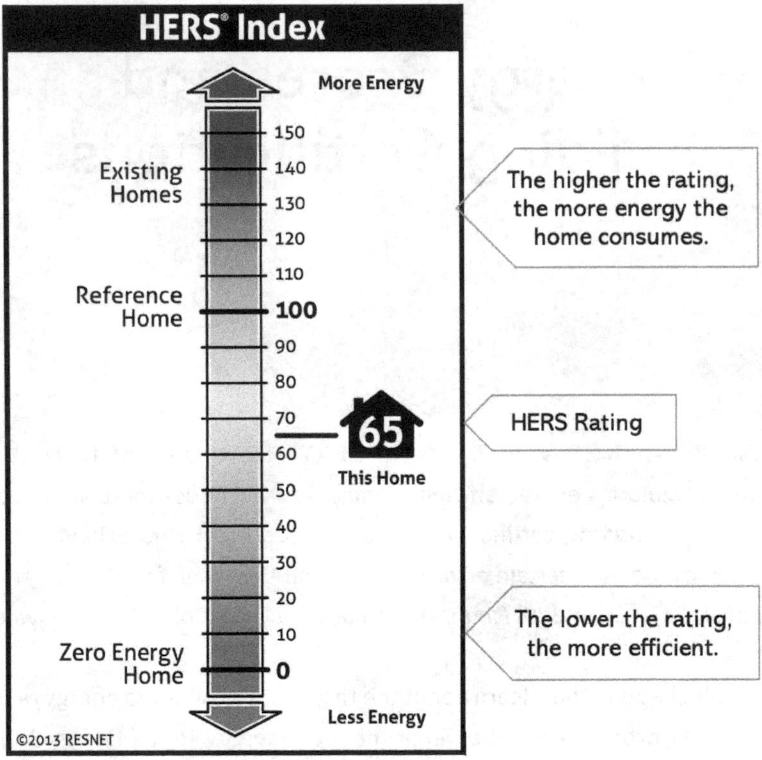

Variables Included in an Energy Rating [140]

- All exterior walls (both above and below grade)
- Floors over unconditioned spaces (garages or basements)
- Ceilings and roofs
- Attics, foundations, and crawlspace
- Windows and doors, vents, and ductwork
- HVAC system, water heating system, and thermostat
- Air leakage of the home
- Leakage in the heating and cooling distribution system

A certified RESNET Home Energy Rater will visit the home and test each area of the home using a series of diagnostic testing equipment to measure the efficiency levels. Based on testing results, the rater will assign a relative performance score (the HERS Index Score). Data is compared to a "reference home," which is the same type, size, and shape of your home. According to RESNET, the typical resale home scores 130 on the HERS Index. Following are examples of what the scores means:[141]

HERS Rating	What it Means
150	Home is 50% less energy efficient than a standard new home.
100	Home is the same level as a standard new home, which is the current industry standard for energy efficiency.
60	Home has made good progress toward optimizing energy performance
30	Home is 70% more efficient than a standard new home, and 100% more efficient than a typical re-sale home.
0	The home is considered a net zero energy home.

RESNET Water Efficiency Rating System

HERS-H20 is a system for rating whole-house water efficiency that includes both indoor and outdoor uses. The system provides a rating on a scale from 0 to 100+ where lower numbers mean less water use. The HERS-H20 Index was developed as part of a partnership between RESNET and the International Code Council (ICC), the Natural Resource Defense Council, and the EPA WaterSense Program.[142]

RESNET Official Website
www.resnet.us

Canada EnerGuide Energy Efficiency Home Evaluation

Natural Resources of Canada administers a home evaluation program that provides homeowners with a comprehensive assessment for new purchase or renovations. Authorized energy advisors and service providers complete assessments. The EnerGuide rating label is shown, along with infographics added by the author.[143]

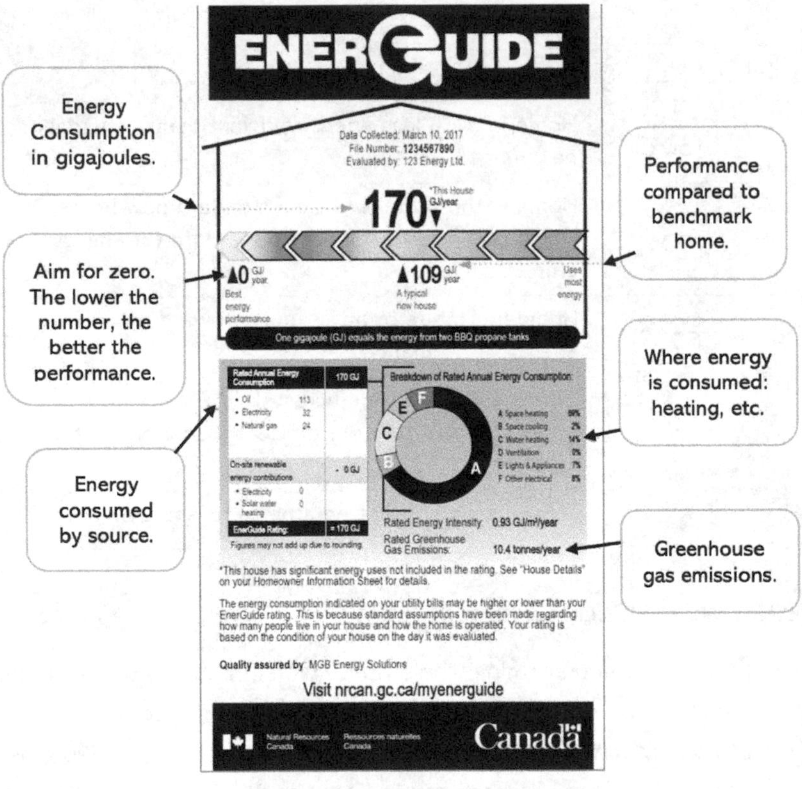

Image source: Natural Resources Canada

How to Understand the EnerGuide Rating, Scale, and Label

The EnerGuide Rating (noted as 170 on the above illustration) demonstrates the energy performance of the home. It is an estimate of the net amount of energy your house consumes in a year.

Performance (noted as 109 on the illustration) shows how the home compares to a home with similar characteristics and property location, known as a "benchmark" home. The lower the number—the better the performance. "Aim toward zero" is the recommendation.

Energy consumed by source (square box on the left side of the label) breaks down the energy of the home consumed by source, such as oil, electricity or natural gas.

Where energy is consumed (circle chart on the right side of the label) shows the proportion of energy consumed, expressed as a percentage and by letter code:

A. Space Heating
B. Space Cooling
C. Water Heating
D. Ventilation
E. Lights and Appliances
F. Other Electrical

The home's impact on the environment (located at the bottom of the circle chart) shows the home's Greenhouse Gas Emissions. The figure in the sample label indicates 10.4 tonnes/year.

Natural Resources Canada provides extensive information for consumers on the main EnerGuide webpage, including detailed instructions on how to prepare for an evaluation; what to expect; what to do the day of your evaluation; and how to interpret the results. Instructions address both home purchases and renovation projects.

EnerGuide Energy Efficiency Home Evaluations
https://www.nrcan.gc.ca/energy-efficiency/energuide/energuide-energy-efficiency-home-evaluations/20552#2

U.S. Department of Energy—Home Energy Score

The Home Energy Score is a tool to help homeowners gain useful information about their home's energy use, and on an assessment by a qualified energy rater. The Home Energy Score uses a simple 1 through 10 scale where a 10 represents the most energy-efficient homes. The report estimates home energy use, associated costs, and provides cost-effective solutions.

The energy efficiency score is based on the home's envelope (foundation, roof, walls, insulation, windows) and heating, cooling, and hot water systems. The report illustrates the home's total energy use estimate, as well as estimates by fuel type and recommendations for cost-effective improvements and associated annual cost savings estimates.

"Score with improvements" reflects the home's expected score if cost-effective improvements are implemented. Illustrated on the following pages are the entire six pages of a sample report.[144]

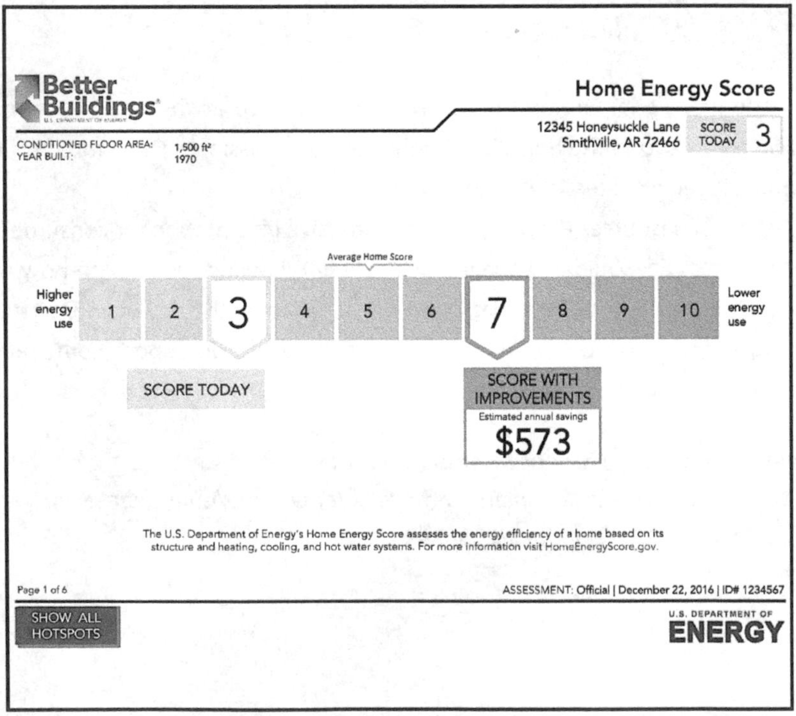

Image source: U.S. Department of Energy

Better Buildings®
U.S. DEPARTMENT OF ENERGY

Home Energy Score

12345 Honeysuckle Lane
Smithville, AR 72466

SCORE TODAY **3**

Home Facts

The Home Energy Score's Home Facts includes details about the home's current structure, systems, and estimated energy use. For more information about how the score is calculated, visit our website at HomeEnergyScore.gov.

About This Home

ASSESSMENT	
Type	Official
Assessor ID	#1234567
Scoring tool version	v2016
HOME CONSTRUCTION	
Year built	1970
Number of bedrooms	3
Stories above ground level	1
Interior floor-to-ceiling height	10
Conditioned floor area	1,500 ft²
Direction faced by front of house	North
Air sealed?	No
Air leakage rate	6,500 CFM50

Estimated Annual Energy Use

ENERGY BY TYPE	
Total	204 MBtus
Score basis	141 MBtus
Electricity	11,956 kWh
Natural gas	519 therms
Propane	226 gallons
COST BASIS	
Electricity	$0.091 / kWh
Natural gas	$1.153 / therms
Propane	$2.171 / gallon
Energy cost per square foot	$1.45 / ft²
DEFINITIONS & CONVERSIONS	
MBtu	Million British thermal units; generic energy unit
kWh	Kilowatt-hour; electricity unit
Therm	100,000 Btu; heat energy unit
Electricity conversion	1 MBtu = 293 kWh
Heat conversion	1 MBtu = 10 therms

Page 2 of 6

ASSESSMENT: Official | December 22, 2016 | ID# 1234567

U.S. DEPARTMENT OF
ENERGY

Image source: U.S. Department of Energy

Better Buildings
U.S. DEPARTMENT OF ENERGY

Home Energy Score

12345 Honeysuckle Lane
Smithville, AR 72466

SCORE TODAY **3**

Home Facts

The Home Energy Score's Home Facts includes details about the home's current structure, systems, and estimated energy use. For more information about how the score is calculated, visit our website at HomeEnergyScore.gov.

Roof / Attic

ROOF / ATTIC 1	
Attic floor area	500 ft²
Roof construction	Roof with Radiant Barrier / Composition Shingles or Metal / R-0
Roof color	Medium dark
Attic: ceiling type	Unconditioned attic
Attic floor insulation	R-25

ROOF / ATTIC 2	
Attic floor area	1,000 ft²
Roof construction	Standard Roof / Composition Shingles or Metal / R-0
Roof color	Medium dark
Attic: ceiling type	Unconditioned attic
Attic floor insulation	R-9

Foundation

FOUNDATION / FLOOR 1	
Floor area	500 ft²
Foundation type	Slab-on-grade foundation
Foundation walls insulation	R-0

FOUNDATION / FLOOR 2	
Floor area	1,000 ft²
Foundation type	Unconditioned basement
Floor insulation above foundation	R-0
Foundation walls insulation	R-0

Walls

WALL CONSTRUCTION	TYPE / EXTERIOR FINISH	INSULATION VALUE
Front	Wood frame with Optimum Value Engineering (OVE) / Brick Veneer	R-19
Back	Wood frame / Wood, Asbestos, Fiber Cement, Shingle, or Masonite	R-0
Right	Concrete block or stone / Stucco	R-3
Left	Wood frame with rigid foam sheathing / aluminum siding	R-3

Page 3 of 6

ASSESSMENT: Official | December 22, 2016 | ID# 1234567

U.S. DEPARTMENT OF
ENERGY

Image source: U.S. Department of Energy

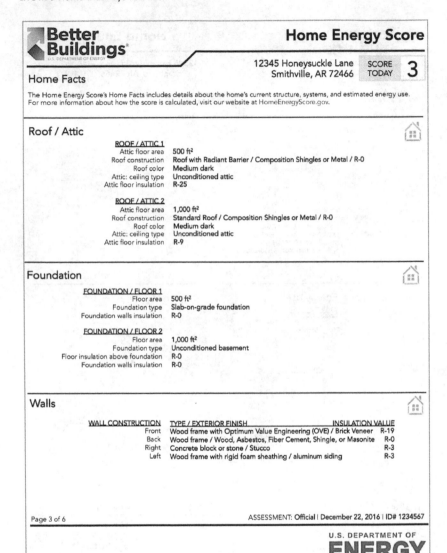

Better Buildings®
U.S. DEPARTMENT OF ENERGY

Home Energy Score

12345 Honeysuckle Lane
Smithville, AR 72466

SCORE TODAY 3

Home Facts

The Home Energy Score's Home Facts includes details about the home's current structure, systems, and estimated energy use. For more information about how the score is calculated, visit our website at HomeEnergyScore.gov.

Windows & Skylights

WINDOW AREA	
Front	70 ft^2
Back	90 ft^2
Right	40 ft^2
Left	30 ft^2

WINDOW CONSTRUCTION	PANES	FRAME	GLAZING or U-VALUE & SHGC
Front	Single	Aluminum	Clear
Back	Double	Wood or Vinyl	Solar-controlled low-E
Right	Double	Aluminum w/ thermal break	Insulating low-E, argon gas fill
Left	Triple	Wood or vinyl	Insulating low-E, argon gas fill

SKYLIGHTS ROOF / ATTIC 1			
Present?	Yes		
Area	30 ft^2		
Type	Single	Aluminum	Tinted

SKYLIGHTS ROOF / ATTIC 2	
Present?	No

Page 4 of 6

ASSESSMENT: Official | December 22, 2016 | ID# 1234567

U.S. DEPARTMENT OF ENERGY

draft

Image source: U.S. Department of Energy

Better Buildings®
U.S. DEPARTMENT OF ENERGY

Home Energy Score

12345 Honeysuckle Lane
Smithville, AR 72466

SCORE TODAY **3**

Home Facts

The Home Energy Score's Home Facts includes details about the home's current structure, systems, and estimated energy use. For more information about how the score is calculated, visit our website at HomeEnergyScore.gov.

Systems

HVAC SYSTEM 1	
Percent conditioned area served	33%
Heating type	Electric heat pump
Heating efficiency value	7.8 HSPF
Cooling type	Electric heat pump
Cooling efficiency value	12 SEER

DUCT SYSTEM 1	INSULATED?	SEALED?	PERCENT OF DUCTS IN THIS LOCATION
Unconditioned attic	Yes	No	100%

HVAC SYSTEM 2	
Percent conditioned area served	67%
Heating type	Central gas furnace
Heating installation year	2009
Cooling type	Central air conditioning
Cooling installation year	2009

DUCT SYSTEM 2	INSULATED?	SEALED?	PERCENT OF DUCTS IN THIS LOCATION
Unconditioned basement	No	No	50%
Unconditioned attic	No	No	25%
Conditioned space	No	No	25%

HOT WATER	
System type	LPG storage
Installation year	1997

Page 5 of 6

ASSESSMENT: Official | December 22, 2016 | ID# 1234567

U.S. DEPARTMENT OF ENERGY

Image source: U.S. Department of Energy

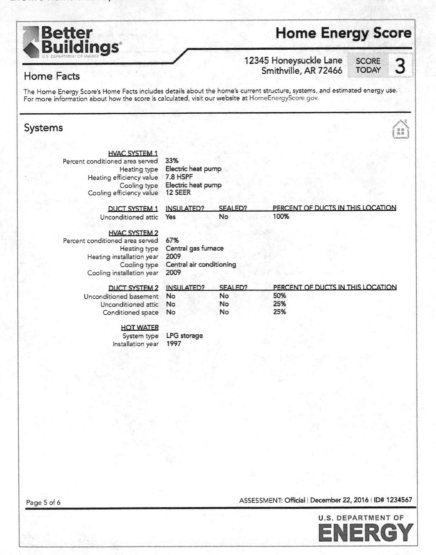

Better Buildings
U.S. DEPARTMENT OF ENERGY

Home Energy Score

12345 Honeysuckle Lane
Smithville, AR 72466

SCORE TODAY **3**

Recommendations

The Home Energy Score's Recommendations show how to improve the energy efficiency of the home to achieve a higher score and save money. When making energy related upgrades, homeowners should consult with a certified energy professional or other technically qualified contractor to ensure proper sizing, installation, safety, and adherence to code. Learn more at HomeEnergyScore.gov.

REPAIR NOW. These improvements will save you money, conserve energy, and improve your comfort.

- **Air Tightness:** Have a professional seal all the gaps and cracks that leak air to save $110 / year
- **Ducts 1:** Add insulation around ducts in unconditioned spaces to at least R-6 to save $43 / year
- **Attic 2:** Increase attic floor insulation to at least R-19 to save $57 / year
- **Ducts 2:** Add insulation around ducts in unconditioned spaces to at least R-6 to save $23 / year
- **Ducts 2:** Have a professional seal all the gaps and cracks that leak air to save $74 / year

REPLACE LATER. These improvements will help you save energy when it's time to replace or upgrade.

- **Windows:** Choose those with an ENERGY STAR label to save $61 / year
- **Water Heater:** Choose one with an ENERGY STAR label to save $159 / year
- **Electric Heat Pump:** Choose one with an ENERGY STAR label to save $32 / year

Comments

Current local incentives may make this house a good candidate for a new water heater.

Page 6 of 6

ASSESSMENT: **Official** | **December 22, 2016** | **ID# 1234567**

U.S. DEPARTMENT OF
ENERGY

Image source: U.S. Department of Energy

Resources:

U.S. Department of Energy Home Energy Score
https://betterbuildingssolutioncenter.energy.gov/home-energy-score

Homeowner Resources
Includes look-up tool for an assessor in your location
https://betterbuildingssolutioncenter.energy.gov/home-energy-score/homeowner-resources

Homeowner Guide
https://betterbuildingssolutioncenter.energy.gov/sites/default/files/attachments/HES_Homeowner_05192016.pdf

Building Certifications

There are many esteemed institutes that specialize in drafting building standards for residential property developers, and their certification programs offer an important badge of quality to a home. An institute's building standards are often adopted by building societies and trade associations.

Independent home builders and contractors have the opportunity to construct an individual home in accordance with a specific certification program. Homes are assessed for compliance to construction and energy performance standards by a professional rater.

Real estate developers who construct a large number of homes can build homes in accordance with a certain standard—and within that standard homebuyers can optionally upgrade to higher levels of performance. As an example, options for homes within one community may be offered as "LEED Silver or Gold." Although all homes are built "above code" and include high-performance features, upgrade options give homebuyers a chance to save money upfront. Homes are designed to easily accommodate the upgrades in the future.

Listed are the foremost building certification programs associated with green-building standards and energy-efficient homes:

Leadership in Energy and Environmental Design (LEED)
U.S. Green Building Council (USGBC)

The LEED rating system was established in 1993 by USGBC. Homes are constructed by builders according to green building standards classified as Silver, Platinum and Gold. The newest programs aimed to reduce greenhouse gas emissions are known as "LEED Zero" and "LEED Positive." LEED is the most widely used green building rating system in the world. LEED provides a framework to create healthy, highly efficient and cost-saving green buildings. Designed and built for performance, every LEED home is third-party-inspected, tested and verified. https://www.usgbc.org

National Green Building Standard (NGBS)

The National Green Building Standard (NGBS) provides practices for the design, construction, and certification of new single-family homes, duplexes, and townhouses. The program is used in partnership with the National Association of Home Builders (NAHB), American Society of Heating, Refrigerating, and Air-Conditioning Engineers (ASHRAE), and International Code Council (ICC). Programs include high-performance levels of Bronze, Silver, Gold, and Emerald. Certification is completed by Home Innovation Research Labs. In October 2020, the 250,000th home was NGBS was certified by Home Innovation Research Labs. https://www.ngbs.com

PHIUS Passive Building Standard

The Passive House Institute US (PHIUS) is a nonprofit organization committed to high-performance passive buildings. PHIUS trains and certifies professionals, maintains the PHIUS+ climate-specific building standard, certifies buildings, and conducts research. PHIUS administers a number of protocols for home and building materials certification, and provides other services through the Passive House Alliance (PHAUS). https://www.phius.org

BREEAM and BRE Global

BREEAM (Building Research Establishment's Environmental Assessment Method) is the world's leading sustainability assessment method for master-planned communities and services more than 80 countries. BRE Global provides independent third-party certifications. https://www.breeam.com

International Living Future Institute (ILFI)

The International Living Future Institute is an international organization that administers a number of certification programs for environmentally responsible building. Each certification path requires fulfillment of key imperatives. Projects include the Core Green Building Certification, Zero Energy, Zero Carbon, Petal, and Living Building Challenge. https://living-future.org

Canadian Home Builders' Association (CHBA)

CHBA represents 9,000 companies and has served as the voice of Canada's residential construction industry since 1943. CHBA provides education and support services for building codes, home labeling programs, and programs such as Energy Star homes, Net Zero, and R-2000. CHBA's Net Zero Energy Housing Council is a collaboration of home builders, manufacturers, design experts, government agencies, utilities, and service providers. The Council's supports innovation, helps define Net Zero Energy (NZE) Technical Requirements, develops standards for licensed third-party Energy Advisors. https://www.chba.ca

Canada Green Building Council

Members of the Canada Green Building Council are companies, institutions, universities, organizations, municipalities, and government agencies involved in the planning, design, construction, maintenance, and operation of buildings, homes, and communities. The Council implemented the "R-2000" program in 1982 to promote sustainability. The Council has adapted the LEED rating system for Canadian circumstances. https://www.cagbc.org

Passive House Canada

Passive House Canada's mission is to make the International Passive House standard of building performance understood and achievable, and to see it adopted by government, industry professionals, and homeowners across Canada through education, advocacy, events, and building projects. The Passive House Building Certification is the internationally recognized building certification system, providing third-party verification and a stamp of quality assurance that a building meets the high performance and comfort levels of the Passive House standard. One important aspect is the process-oriented approach to certification. Once this approach is implemented, various audits can be done to ensure levels are met. There are five levels of certification, including a program for retrofits.
https://www.passivehousecanada.com/passive-house-building-certification/

CHAPTER 6

Home Building Opportunities

YOU CAN BUILD YOUR DREAM HOME ON YOUR OWN LAND. If you own land, or are able to purchase a buildable lot, there is a growing number of opportunities for building your own home. This is in part due to significant advancements made in the prefabricated home building industry. According to Business Wire, "The single-family modular and prefabricated housing construction global market is expected to reach $100.07 billion in 2023."[145]

Also referred to as "factory-built homes," most of the work is completed in a climate-controlled manufacturing facility. Such facilities have proven to be a safer environment for workers and provide manufacturers with greater controls for production and delivery timeframes.

Today's prefabricated home-building materials are durable, non-toxic, sustainably sourced, and designed for optimum energy efficiency. You will find homes that are Energy Star Certified, as well as homes ready for Net Zero and Zero Carbon.

This chapter features several types of homes that are fully—or partially—built in an off-site facility. In some cases, you will have the option to roll up your sleeves and be the general contractor in building your own home.

Modular Homes

According to the National Modular Housing Council, modular housing is one of the fastest growing sectors of the construction industry.[146] Due to the increasing role of factory-built modular construction in Canada's building industry, in 2017, members of the Canadian Manufactured Housing Institute and MHI Canada joined forces to create the Canadian Home Builders' Association (CHBA) Modular Construction Council.[147]

Many modular home builders offer upscale, high-end designs and a wide choice of architectural options. Styles range from mid-century modern to traditional farmhouses with porches. Once finished, it is hard to distinguish the property from a custom-built home.

Shutterstock Images

Generally, about two-thirds of modular home construction is completed at the factory. Homes are transported to the building site in "modules" and assembled by an authorized construction team.

Usually, homebuyers hire a local builder to serve as the general contractor, who completes remaining tasks such as plumbing, electric, and finishing. This is known as "buttoning up." Dealers generally give homebuyers the option of either having windows and other fixtures included, or buying them from a local supply company.

Modular and prefabricated home descriptions are often used interchangeably, but they are not identical. According to Metal Building Homes, "Prefab is actually an umbrella that includes modular houses as well as those built using other methods such as panel construction and steel frame design. If any part of the house has been manufactured in advance at a factory before it is shipped to the site, that house is defined as prefabricated."[148]

There are also differences between manufactured homes and modular homes. Manufactured homes must conform to a national building code, while modular homes must conform to state and local zoning laws. Most mortgage lenders offer specific types of loans for manufactured homes. However, modular homes are classified the same as general home construction home, known as "stick-built."

Manufactured Homes

According to the report, *2020 Manufactured Housing Facts* from the Manufactured Housing Institute (MHI), 22 million people in America live in manufactured homes. In 2019, over 94,615 manufactured homes were produced at 129 manufacturing plants. Manufactured homes have an average sales price of $78,500 and cost less than half as much as a site-built homes.[149]

The Manufactured Housing Institute states, "Today's manufactured homes have experienced an evolution. Greater flexibility in the construction process allows for customization of each home to meet a buyer's lifestyle and needs. Interior features include vaulted ceilings, working fireplaces, state-of-the-art kitchens and baths, and porches."

> An Energy Star certified manufactured home is a home that has been designed, produced, and installed by the home manufacturer to meet Energy Star requirements for energy efficiency. Each Energy Star certified manufactured home is inspected while it's being built in the factory and during onsite installation to verify it meets Energy Star standards.[150]
>
> —Energy Star

Shutterstock Images

Over the past 20 years, manufacturers have significantly expanded the range of architectural home styles and floor plan options. Traditionally, manufactured homes are built in communities, and the land is included in the purchase price. Due to the significant cost savings, homebuyers are buying their own lots and choosing a manufactured home over a stick-built home.

Authorized dealers generally handle the purchase agreement, and follow through with the buyer regarding building permits, site preparation, and delivery logistics. Although a number of manufactured home dealers have showrooms, many buyers begin their search on the Internet.

Today's shopping experience can take online viewers through a three-dimensional tour of a multi-story "dollhouse." Most websites include videos of finished homes, as well as displaying choices for cabinetry, tiles, bath and kitchen fixtures, exterior colors, and architectural features.

Manufactured homes in the United States must be built in accordance with laws governed by the U.S. Department of Housing and Urban Development. Homebuyers have more financing flexibility if the home is certified as *MH Advantage*. In Canada, factory-built homes and foundations must be in compliance with national and provincial building codes.

Shutterstock Images

Prefab Home Kits

Prefab kits are sustainably built, affordable, and available for quick delivery to your site. Many types of homes can be installed on a steel chassis, and do not require a permanent foundation.

Manufacturers generally offer a "turnkey" buying option, and assembly is completed on your land lot by the manufacturer's team. Some home types can be built by the homebuyer. Plumbing and electrical wiring, however, must be completed by licensed contractors. You will find kits described as any of the following:

- Accessory dwelling units (ADUs)
- Barndominiums
- Cantilevers
- Chalets or A-frames
- Eco-homes
- Geodesic domes
- Log cabins
- Mobile or moveable
- Post and beam barns
- Shipping containers
- Steel boxes or steel cabins
- Tiny homes

Depending on the house size, type of foundation, and local zoning rules, you will most likely need a building permit. The prefab dealer will explain requirements for preparing the land, and if applicable, constructing the foundation. Some local zoning laws do not require building permits for tiny homes with square footage under a specified limit. Permit classifications can also vary for mobile or moveable dwellings.

Chapter 8, *Mortgage Financing,* summarizes the various types of pricing structures for prefab kits, as well as explains "chattel mortgages," which is the type of funding that is available on mobile homes and other properties that are not situated on permanent foundations.

Prefab Kits from ECOHome

ECOHome of Canada is a team of engineers, environmentalists, and former home builders committed to providing homeowners and builders with essential information for creating more sustainable, durable, and healthier homes.

ECOHome represents architects and manufacturers who design and build high-end, energy-efficient prefab homes. Homes are ideal for northeastern climates and designed with maximum efficiency and low energy consumption. ECOHomes are made with healthy and renewable Canadian construction materials and are LEED-ready, with some models suitable for a Zero Energy rating or Passive House certification.

Homes are available in kit form or fully built, and can be shipped to most locations in the U.S. and Canada. Two models are shown on the following page.

Photo credit: ECOHome

The Charlevoix

LEED-ready, craftsman style prefab home kit. Classic house design with traditional accents. Materials carefully chosen for healthy indoor air quality and durability. Two floors plus walk-out basement. 2,310 square feet.

Photo credit: ECOHome

Eco-Habitat S1600

Modern prefab family eco home with architecture that focuses on energy-efficient solar gain. Reinforced insulation, low environmental footprint, healthy materials for optimum indoor air quality. Low carbon design with lowest operating costs possible. 3 bedrooms, 2 floors, 1,600 square feet.

Log and Timber Homes

Log homes are a time-honored tradition and considered to be one of the most sustainable forms of construction. Wood provides excellent thermal conductivity, keeping the warm air inside the home and the cool air outside.

According to the North American Forest Products Industry, "In a wood building, the carbon is kept out of the atmosphere for the lifetime of the structure. Wood stores more carbon than is emitted during its harvest, production, transport, and installation—even when transported over great distances." Since wood is a lighter building material, log and timber frame homes require less reinforcing steel and smaller footings, thereby reducing carbon emissions.[151]

Photo credit: Heidi Long, Longviews Studios, Inc.

The house pictured above was the first log home to pass the strict energy codes of Vail, Colorado. Built with high-efficiency commercial-grade windows and other energy features, the home is powered by a free-standing array of solar panels that are mounted on the ground next to the house. In addition to solar energy, this remote mountaintop home also has back-up generators. On the next page is a photo of the home's magnificent interior.

Photo credit: Heidi Long, Longviews Studios, Inc.

Photo Credit: Heidi Long, Longviews Studios, Inc.

The 160-year-old, 900-square-foot homestead cabin shown above was the first LEED Platinum certification in Montana, and is believed to be the oldest LEED Platinum project in the nation. The cabin was moved to its current location, and the exterior walls were split and filled with insulation. Original features include beadboard cabinets, and doors and roofing from reclaimed materials, and the original Majestic stove was refurbished to Energy Star standards. All materials were sourced within 500 miles of the site.

Many log home manufacturing companies have been building homes for generations. Known for providing good old-fashioned customer service, tried-and-true methods are shared with customers, along with detailed instructions and specifications for professional contractors.

> Homebuyers now have the opportunity to have energy efficient features while enjoying the rustic elegance of exposed timber. Hidden behind walls of authentic half logs and decorative finishes, the latest insulated materials and components are employed to deliver maximum comfort and energy performance.
>
> —Donna Peak, Editor-in-Chief, *Log & Timber Home Living* magazine

Log &Timber Home Living magazine shares three important "green" benefits to building a log and timber home:[152]

1. Logs and timbers aren't overly processed, and there is much less waste material (i.e., scrap wood and sawdust) generated than it takes to make 2x4s and 2x6s, thereby reducing the life-cycle carbon footprint.
2. The larger the log, the more thermal mass it generates. Thermal mass allows an object to collect and store the sun's radiant heat, and then disperse it slowly over time. This attribute lets log homes stay cooler in the summer and warmer in the winter, a phenomenon that can't be achieved with manufactured insulation.
3. Most timber-frame homes are constructed with enclosed insulated panel systems, increasing energy efficiency. Typically, panels are comprised of a solid foam core sandwiched between oriented strand boards (OSBs), which are also green. Insulation is continuous, without interruption by 2x6 studs, contributing to exceptionally high R-values and unparalleled energy efficiency.

There are basic steps for purchasing a log home from a dealer, as explained by Dan Mitchell, owner of Eagle CDI in Seymour, Tennessee, and a professor at Log and Timber Home University:

> "Log packages are the starting point of log homes and constitute the bulk of building materials needed. Packages vary among manufacturers, and are comprised of three components: walls only, structural shell, or a complete package. When comparison shopping, it's important to gather a complete list of materials and associated costs for each item included in the package."[153]

Log and Timber Home Living Magazine offers a full range of resources on its website, where you can view home models and floor plans from dozens of log home builders. You'll find a full range of purchase and construction options, as well as information regarding the manufacturer's environmental and reforestation policies.

Resources:

Log and Timber Home University. If you're considering buying a log and timber home, Log and Timber Home University offers on-line courses taught by home-building experts. Courses include "Dream and Design," as well as courses on planning, building, and maintaining your home.
https://www.creativehomeclasses.com

Log & Timber Home Living
https://www.loghome.com

ECOHome
https://www.ecohome.net

ManufacturedHomes.com
https://www.manufacturedhomes.com/manufacturers

Metal Building Homes
https://metalbuildinghomes.org/

Prefab Review
https://www.prefabreview.com

Log and Timber Home Council (NAHB)
https://www.nahb.org/subsites/log-homes

International Log Builders' Association (Canada)
https://logassociation.org

Land Watch (Find land in U.S.)
https://www.landwatch.com/land

Land Sale Listings (Find land in Canada)
https://www.landsalelistings.com/canada/

CHAPTER 7

Healthy Homes

SMART HOME SYSTEMS ARE GOOD FOR HEALTH AND SAFETY. People today have many ways to monitor their home electronically. Products include thermostats that can adjust the temperature of your home when it senses your car is 10 miles away, as mentioned earlier in Chapter 2. Some solar photovoltaic systems include a mobile app, enabling homeowners to monitor solar energy production while they are away.

Smart home technology helps conserve water, reduce energy costs, and keep your home comfortable. In this chapter, we cover a different aspect of smart home technology—monitoring and detection for health and safety.

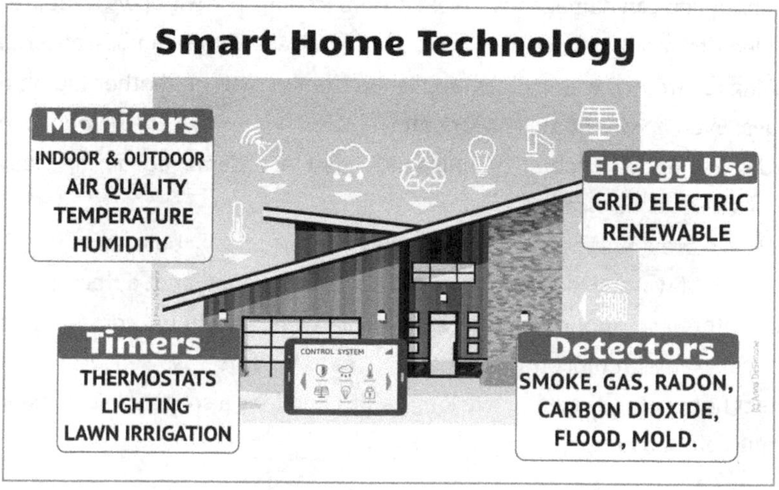

The most well-known health and safety monitors are for detecting smoke, fire, and carbon dioxide. Thanks to scientific advancement, there are even more ways you can protect everyone in your household—including pets—from exposure to harmful toxins and pollutants.

Many innovative products are built with professional-grade sensors and are able to continuously monitor indoor and outdoor temperature, humidity, air pressure, oxygen levels, pollen, and particulate matter.

Air quality monitors are built with "particle detectors," which sense the size of a particle. To assess air quality, a total count of the number of particles is made within a target area of a specific size. Portable devices, however, are not able to differentiate particles by type, such as pollen vs. cat dander. They do monitor humidity, however, and some devices are able to determine mold risk.

Portable brands include *Airthings Wave, Awair Element, Ecowitt, EG Air Quality Monitor, Eve Room Indoor Air Quality Monitor, Foobot, IQAir, Kaiterra Laser Egg+Chemical Indoor Air Quality Monitor,* and *uHoo Indoor Air Quality Sensor.* Products often pair with smart home systems such as *Amazon Alexa, Apple HomeKit, ecobee, and Google Home.*

Flood Sensors

Floods and water leaks in your home can be serious. Even smaller leaks that go unnoticed can damage your walls, floors, ceilings, or windows. Wet areas can lead to mold, discussed in more detail below. Floods can be caused by leaking (or frozen) water pipes, appliance breakdowns, and other plumbing issues. Even if your home is adequately sealed, water can enter your home through windows, doors, or bulkheads that are damaged during heavy storms such as hurricanes.

There are a number of electronic devices specifically built to detect the presence of water. Flood alarms come in two categories, spot detectors, and area detectors. "Spot detectors" emit an alarm signal when it comes into direct contact with moisture or water. "Area detectors" use sensor wires to detect floods. They usually have long cables and may also include extensions to multiple sensors.

An "active" flood alarm is a device that is connected to water pumps or pipes. When the sensor is triggered, the water supply is shut off. "Passive" detection systems work best when placed in strategic locations where there may be a risk of flooding, such as the basement, laundry room, or under the kitchen sink.

There are a number of devices that can be paired with your smart home system so that you can be alerted by text or email, in addition to the alarm signal. Brands include *FIBARO, First Alert, La Homieta, LeakSmart, Martika Signal, Samsung SmartThings,* and *Watchdog.*

Biological Pollutants

Biological contaminants include dust, dander, pollen, bacteria, mold, mildew, and viruses. As explained in the *Indoor Air Quality* section in Chapter 2, whole-house air-filtering and ventilation systems can significantly improve your home's air quality.

Whole-house air-filtering systems are very powerful and can serve as a year-round defense from a broad range of biological pollutants and other airborne irritants including mold spores, allergens, bacteria, viruses, dander, dust, dust mites, pests, and smog.

Systems are duct-based and integrated within the HVAC furnace. Whole-house systems must be professionally installed and may be equipped with a variety of filter types. Some types of filter require more frequent replacement, and some require maintenance. High-efficiency particulate air filters, known as HEPA, are able to capture dust, dander, pollen, and other biological pollutants.

Ultraviolet (UV) filters are able to extinguish mold, fungus, and bacteria. Filters that incorporate an electrostatic precipitation process will emit an electrical charge, effectively zapping the particle. *(Note: a complete listing of filter types and efficiency ratings is provided on the chart in the Indoor Air Quality section in Chapter 2.)*

Whole-house air-filtering brands include *Amaircare 10000, Aprilaire, Beyond by Aerus, Honeywell, Lennox PureAir, IQAir,* and *Rheem RXIE.*

Mold

Mold is a critical biological contaminant since it can release disease-causing toxins. Symptoms of health problems caused by biological pollutants include sneezing, watery eyes, coughing, shortness of breath, dizziness, lethargy, fever and digestive problems.[154]

According to the Environmental Protection Agency, mold spores waft through the indoor and outdoor air continually. When mold spores land on a damp spot indoors, they may begin growing and digesting whatever they are growing on in order to survive.

There are many types of mold, and none of them will grow without water or moisture. Mold can grow on wood, paper, carpet, and foods. If excessive moisture or water accumulates indoors, mold growth will often occur, particularly if the moisture problem remains undiscovered or was not addressed.[155] *(Note: steps to control moisture and prevent mold are outlined in* the Thermal Enclosure *section of Chapter 2.)*

> **There is no practical way to eliminate all mold and mold spores in the indoor environment. The way to control mold growth is to control moisture.**
>
> —Environmental Protection Agency

Environmental Toxins

According to the World Health Organization (WHO), 24% of all global deaths are linked to the environment. In recent history, many housing laws were enacted to protect consumers from environmental toxins. In the residential home building industry, the use of lead, lead-based paint, asbestos, mercury, and other substances has been severely restricted or prohibited.

There are a few air-quality monitoring systems that can detect certain toxins. However, using specialized detection equipment can provide greater reliability and assurance. In fact, some detection systems are required by law. Requirements for detection systems in residential apartments or homes for smoke, carbon dioxide and radon are established by state or provincial law.

Radon

According to the Environmental Protection Agency (EPA), radon is a cancer-causing, radioactive gas. You can't see, taste, or smell radon—but when you breathe air containing radon, you can get lung cancer. In fact, the Surgeon General has warned that radon is the second leading cause of lung cancer in the United States today. Only smoking causes more lung cancer deaths.[156]

> **Radon comes from the natural decay of uranium found in nearly all soils. It typically moves up through the ground to the air above and into your home through cracks and other holes in the foundation.**
>
> —Environmental Protection Agency

Radon can be found throughout the United States. Any home may have a radon problem, including new and old homes, well-sealed and well-ventilated homes, and homes with or without basements. Radon becomes trapped inside the home, where it can build up. Radon can enter through well water."[157]

The EPA and the U.S. Surgeon General recommend testing in all homes below the third floor. The EPA guideline is that a "radon reduction system" must be installed when the test results indicate a level greater than 4 pCi/L (or picocuries) per liter of air. A radon reduction system is often referred to as "mitigation," and can reduce levels in a home up to 99%.

New homes can be built with "radon-resistant construction" features. These techniques can be effective in preventing radon entry, as well as reducing radon levels in the home. Installing them at the time of construction makes it easier and less expensive to reduce levels below the safety requirement.[158]

In today's real estate market, many homebuyers obtain a property inspection on the home which may include a radon test. To determine radon levels, the testing organization places a small device in the basement, or lowest level of the home if there is no basement. After a few days, the testing company returns to collect the device and read the results.

If the test indicates a level greater than 4 pCi/L, the property seller is required to mitigate. Depending upon the property type, there are a number of mitigation approaches that can be completed at relatively low cost. Once the final test indicates success, the home can be considered safe.

> Mitigation techniques involve the use of a vent pipe and fan that creates a negative pressure field. This pulls air out from beneath the foundation, averting potential build-up of radon. The vent stack runs vertically to an exit point above the roof line where the air is safely dissipated.[159]
>
> —Andrew Morrison, DMI AccuSystems

Radon in Canada

According to Health Canada, uranium is a common element found everywhere in Earth's crust. As a result, radon gas can be found throughout Canada. Concentrations differ greatly across the country but are usually higher in areas where there is a higher amount of uranium in underlying rock and soil.[160]

The Public Health Infobase of the Government of Canada reports that, in Canada, radon is the second-highest cause of lung cancer, after smoking. The percentage of homes with high radon levels is presented in the map developed by Colin Gutcher and the radon technical operations group at the Radon Protection Bureau.[161] *(Note: see Resources for web address)*

Carbon Monoxide

According to the Environmental Protection Agency (EPA), carbon monoxide (CO) is a colorless, odorless gas that interferes with the delivery of oxygen throughout the body. At high concentrations it can cause unconsciousness and death. The symptoms of carbon monoxide poisoning are sometimes confused with the flu or food poisoning.

Lower concentrations can cause a range of symptoms, including headaches, dizziness, weakness, nausea, confusion, disorientation, fatigue in healthy people and episodes of increased chest pain in people with chronic heart disease.[162]

Sources of Carbon Monoxide

- Unvented kerosene and gas space heaters
- Leaking chimneys and furnaces
- Back-drafting from furnaces, gas water heaters, wood stoves and fireplaces
- Gas stoves
- Generators and other gasoline-powered equipment
- Automobile exhaust from attached garages
- Tobacco smoke
- Auto, truck, or bus exhaust from attached garages, nearby roads, or parking areas
- Incomplete oxidation during combustion in gas ranges, and unvented gas or kerosene heaters
- Worn or poorly adjusted and maintained combustion devices, such as boilers and furnaces; leaking, improperly sized, blocked, or disconnected flues.

Steps to Reduce Exposure to Carbon Monoxide

The EPA states it is important for combustion equipment to be maintained and properly adjusted. Gas appliances need proper adjustment and exhaust fans vented to the outside. Wood stoves should meet emission standards and have tight-fitting doors. Proper fuel must be used for kerosene space heaters. Ventilation can be used as a temporary measure when high levels of CO are expected for short periods of time.[163]

Carbon Monoxide Guidance from Health Canada

Health Canada advises that carbon monoxide can only be detected with a CO alarm installed in the home. Alarms must be accredited by the Standards Council of Canada and noted with a certification mark such as CSA, UL, Intertek ETL, etc. Alarms have an audible sound to warn you of high CO levels in your home. Health Canada offers the following guidance to prevent carbon monoxide poisoning: [164]

- Prevent indoor smoking.
- Keep the door between your house and the garage closed.
- Do not idle vehicles in the garage, even if the garage door is open.
- Never use gas-powered machines in the garage, such as: trimmers, generators, lawnmowers, or snowblowers.
- Never use a barbecue or portable fuel-burning camping equipment inside a home, garage, vehicle, camper, or tent.
- Never use kerosene or oil space heaters or lamps in enclosed areas unless they're specifically designed for indoor use.
- Make sure appliances, fireplaces, furnaces, and water heaters are well maintained and inspected by a professional.
- During and after a snowstorm, inspect the following exhaust vents to make sure they are not covered with snow: furnace, fireplace, chimney, heat recovery ventilator, wood-burning or gas stove, and clothes dryer.

Nitrogen Dioxide

Nitrogen dioxide (NO_2) is another "combustion gas," that is released from household tobacco smoking, second-hand smoke, gas stoves, kerosene heaters, and vehicle exhaust. Nitrogen dioxide is a reddish-brown gas, whose odor irritates the mucous membranes in the eyes, nose, and throat. It can cause shortness of breath after exposure to high concentrations.

According to the EPA, high concentrations or continued exposure to low levels of nitrogen dioxide can increase the risk of respiratory infection, and elevated levels may lead to the development of lung disease such as emphysema. People at particular risk from exposure to nitrogen dioxide include children and individuals with asthma and other respiratory diseases.[165]

Volatile Organic Compounds (VOCs)

Volatile Organic Compounds (VOCs) represent a large group of human-made and naturally occurring chemicals. Common examples of VOCs include formaldehyde, benzene, xylene, acetaldehyde, toluene, ethylbenzene, and naphthalene. Some are odorless, and concentrations of many VOCs are consistently higher indoors (up to ten times higher) than outdoors.

VOCs are emitted as gases from certain solids or liquids and can have short- and long-term adverse health effects. Symptoms associated with exposure to VOCs include, but are not limited to, eye irritation, nose and throat discomfort, headache, allergic skin reaction, nausea, dizziness, and fatigue.

VOCs are found in paints, lacquers, paint strippers, cleaning supplies, pesticides, building materials, furnishings, office copiers, printers, copy paper, graphics, craft materials, glues, adhesives, permanent markers, correction fluids, photographic solutions, wood preservatives, aerosol sprays, cleaning products, disinfectants, moth repellants, air fresheners, pesticides, dry-cleaned clothing, stored fuels, and automotive products. VOCs are released by these products while they are being used, and to some degree, when they are stored.[166, 167]

The EPA recommends the following steps to reduce exposure to VOCs:

- Increase ventilation when using products that emit VOCs.
- Meet or exceed any label precautions.
- Do not store paints and similar materials inside the home.
- Use integrated pest management techniques to reduce the need for pesticides.
- Use household products according to manufacturer's directions.
- Make sure you provide plenty of fresh air when using products.
- Throw away unused or little-used containers safely; buy in quantities that you will use soon.
- Keep out of reach of children and pets.
- Never mix household care products unless directed on the label.

Formaldehyde

Formaldehyde is a chemical used widely by industry to manufacture building materials and numerous household products. Formaldehyde is a colorless, pungent-smelling gas, and certain levels of exposure can cause watery eyes, burning sensations in the eyes and throat, nausea, and difficulty in breathing. High concentrations may trigger attacks in people with asthma.

In homes, the most significant sources of formaldehyde are pressed wood products made using adhesives containing urea-formaldehyde resins. Pressed wood products made for indoor use include particleboard, shelving, cabinetry, furniture, and paneling. Medium-density fiberboard is considered the highest formaldehyde-emitting pressed wood product.

In addition to building materials, sources of formaldehyde are from smoking and the use of unvented, fuel-burning appliances such as gas stoves or kerosene space heaters.

Household products that contain formaldehyde include glues, paints, coatings, lacquers, finishes, paper products, and permanent-press fabrics. Formaldehyde may be found in cosmetics, fabric softeners, dishwashing liquids, and preservatives used in some medicines.[168, 169]

The EPA states that the best-known VOC is formaldehyde. However, it is one of the few indoor air pollutants that can be readily measured. The EPA recommends that if a source is identified, it can be removed. If it is not possible to remove, exposure can be reduced by using a sealant on all exposed surfaces of paneling and other furnishings.[170]

Asbestos

Asbestos is a mineral fiber that is strong, flexible, resistant to heat and chemical corrosion, and insulates well. These features led to the use of asbestos in up to 3,000 consumer products before government agencies began to phase it out in the 1970s because of its health hazards. Asbestos has been used in insulation, roofing, siding, vinyl floor tiles, fireproofing materials, texturized paint, and soundproofing.[171]

As explained in Chapter 2, certain types of insulation were contaminated with asbestos due to shared manufacturing facilities. If you believe that your home—or a home that you are buying—contains asbestos, the material should not be disturbed. When asbestos is disturbed, the material may release fibers that can be inhaled into the lungs. Refer to resources at the end of this chapter for safe removal of asbestos.

Lead

Until 1978, lead compounds were an important component of many paints. Lead was added to paint to promote adhesion, corrosion control, drying, and covering. Lead-based paint was used extensively on exteriors and interior trim-work, windowsills, sashes, window frames, baseboards, wainscoting, doors, frames, and high-gloss wall surfaces, such as those found in kitchens and bathrooms.[172]

Lead is defined as a soft, heavy, malleable bluish-white metallic element. It has many uses and is found mostly in pipes, cable sheaths, batteries, solder, and shields against radioactivity. It melts easily and quickly, can be molded or shaped into thin sheets, and can be drawn out into wire or threads. Lead also is very resistant to weather conditions.

Lead and lead compounds are toxic and can present a severe hazard to those who are overexposed to them. Lead poses an especially high risk to children, and federal laws require the removal of lead-based paint that is within the reach of children. Laws can apply to apartment rentals and to homes that are purchased. The only way to determine which building components are coated with lead paint is through inspection and testing.

Pesticides

According to the U.S. Department of Housing and Urban Development (HUD), measurable levels of up to a dozen pesticides have been found in the air inside homes. Pesticides used in and around the home include products to control insects, termites, rodents, fungi, and microbes. These products are found in sprays, sticks, powders, crystals, balls, and foggers.

HUD recommends that all pest management options, including natural, biologic, cultural, and chemical methods, should be considered. Those that have the least impact on health and the environment should be selected. Most household pests can be controlled by eliminating the habitat for the pest both inside and outside, building or screening them out, eliminating food and harborage areas, and safely using appropriate pesticides.[173]

In Canada, all pesticides must meet the requirements of the Pest Control Products Act and its regulations. Health Canada regulates pesticides under the authority of the Pest Control Products Act. Products are registered only when scientific evidence confirms that its use will not harm the health and environment of Canadians when it is used as directed on the label.[174]

Protecting Household Pets

According to Animal Wellness, “because dogs and cats are smaller than we are, and tend to spend more time indoors, they are particularly susceptible to health problems that indoor pollution can cause.”

VOCs, especially formaldehyde, have the same health risks to pets as to humans, such as eye, nose, and throat irritation, skin reactions, dizziness, and fatigue. For extra safety, Animal Wellness recommends regularly washing soft toys. Items that can’t be washed can be placed in the freezer for a day or two to kill dust mites.[175]

U.S. Resources

Radon

Information for Individuals and Families; Buyers and Sellers; and Builders. https://www.epa.gov/radon

Radon Maps and State Information

https://www.epa.gov/radon/find-information-about-local-radon-zones-and-state-contact-information

Carbon Monoxide

https://www.epa.gov/indoor-air-quality-iaq/what-carbon-monoxide-0

Nitrogen Dioxide

https://www.epa.gov/no2-pollution/basic-information-about-no2

Volatile Organic Compounds

https://www.epa.gov/indoor-air-quality-iaq/what-are-volatile-organic-compounds-vocs

Asbestos

Protect Your Family section includes information about removal
https://www.epa.gov/asbestos/learn-about-asbestos#asbestos

Lead

https://www.epa.gov/lead

Pesticides

https://www.epa.gov/pesticides

Hayward Healthy Home Testing

Free, on-line assessment and healthy home score. After answering a set of simple questions, an instant intelligence report is provided about your home and issues, along with specific, tailor-made steps, action plan, and guidance. https://www.haywardscore.com

Canada Resources

Radon
https://www.canada.ca/en/health-canada/services/health-risks-safety/radiation/radon.html

Radon Map
https://health-infobase.canada.ca/datalab/radon-blog.html#map

Carbon Monoxide
https://www.canada.ca/en/health-canada/services/air-quality/indoor-air-contaminants/keep-carbon-monoxide-out-your-home.html

Nitrogen Dioxide
https://www.canada.ca/en/health-canada/services/air-quality/indoor-air-contaminants/nitrogen-dioxide.html

Volatile Organic Compounds
https://www.canada.ca/en/health-canada/services/air-quality/indoor-air-contaminants/volatile-organic-compounds.html

Asbestos
https://www.canada.ca/en/health-canada/services/air-quality/indoor-air-contaminants/health-risks-asbestos.html

Lead
https://www.canada.ca/en/health-canada/services/home-safety/lead-based-paint.html

Pesticides
https://www.canada.ca/en/health-canada/services/consumer-product-safety/pesticides-pest-management/public.html

CHAPTER 8

Mortgage Financing

SAVING FOR A DOWN PAYMENT IS THE NUMBER ONE OBSTACLE for homebuyers. If you are able to buy a new energy-efficient home, that's great! Depending upon your local real estate market conditions, however, your options may be somewhat limited. By purchasing an existing home, you still have the chance to have maximum energy efficiency, and with net zero potential. But after covering the down payment and closing costs, you often have little left to pay for energy improvements. You might want to consider a financing option where you can "roll the retrofit costs" into your mortgage.

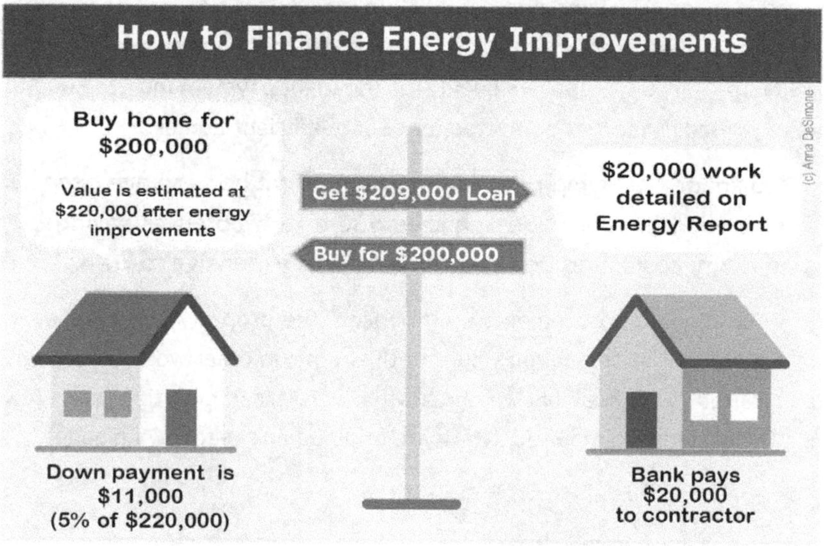
How to Finance Energy Improvements
Buy home for $200,000
Value is estimated at $220,000 after energy improvements
Get $209,000 Loan
Buy for $200,000
$20,000 work detailed on Energy Report
(c) Anna DeSimone
Down payment is $11,000 (5% of $220,000)
Bank pays $20,000 to contractor

The infographic shown on the previous page describes a purchase price of $200,000—and that is the amount the property seller will receive. The closing documents, however, will denote a "transaction cost" of $220,000. Below is a side-by-side comparison between this unique financing option and a traditional mortgage.

	Traditional Mortgage	Roll in Retrofit Costs
Paid to Property Seller	$ 200,000	$ 200,000
Paid to Contractor	0	$ 20,000
Appraisal Valuation	$ 200,000	$ 220,000
5% Down Payment	$ 10,000	$ 11,000
Mortgage Amount	$ 190,000	$ 209,000
Monthly Loan Payment	$ 907	$ 998

Note: mortgage payment is based on 30-year term at 4.00% interest.

In addition to the down payment, there will be closing costs such as lender fees, points, and other settlement charges. The mortgage payment noted is for principal and interest (P&I) only, and does not include monthly escrows such as property taxes, hazard insurance, or mortgage insurance premiums. Most homebuyers qualify for the slight payment increase due to underwriting flexibilities permitted for energy-efficient homes.

Mortgage qualifying rules for energy-efficient homes have been expanded by mortgage agencies due to the potential savings in utility costs, and because they are less expensive to own.

When home improvements are financed, the property appraiser must determine the "as completed value" of the home. In other words, the home is appraised "as if" the work was already done. To accomplish this task, a few additional steps are required, which are outlined on the following pages.

Your first step is to obtain an energy assessment on the home you are buying from a certified energy rater. The image below is a partial section of the *Home Energy Score* report from the Department of Energy, shown earlier in Chapter 5. Note that figures are labelled as "score today" and "score with improvements." If all improvements were completed, the annual estimated savings would be $573.

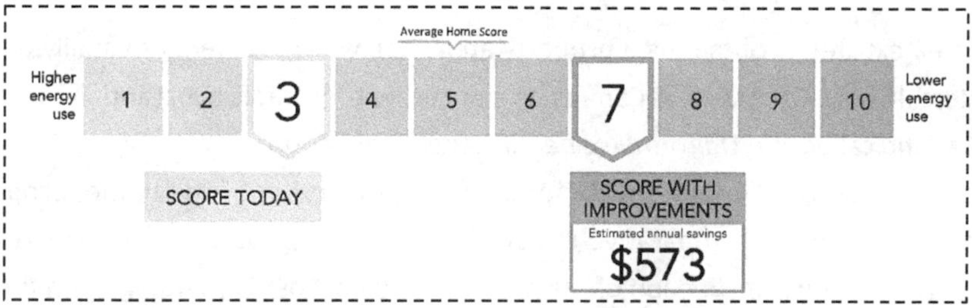

A section from the final page of the same report is shown below. Note that recommendations for improvements are listed as "repair now," or "replace later." Although home energy assessments have varying methodologies and formats, they all include recommendations for upgrades and energy-saving improvements.

REPAIR NOW. These improvements will save you money, conserve energy, and improve your comfort.

- **Air Tightness:** Have a professional seal all the gaps and cracks that leak air to save $110 / year
- **Ducts 1:** Add insulation around ducts in unconditioned spaces to at least R-6 to save $43 / year
- **Attic 2:** Increase attic floor insulation to at least R-19 to save $57 / year
- **Ducts 2:** Add insulation around ducts in unconditioned spaces to at least R-6 to save $23 / year
- **Ducts 2:** Have a professional seal all the gaps and cracks that leak air to save $74 / year

REPLACE LATER. These improvements will help you save energy when it's time to replace or upgrade.

- **Windows:** Choose those with an ENERGY STAR label to save $61 / year
- **Water Heater:** Choose one with an ENERGY STAR label to save $159 / year
- **Electric Heat Pump:** Choose one with an ENERGY STAR label to save $32 / year

Source of above images: U.S. Department of Energy

When you receive your energy report, you will need to provide a copy to your mortgage lender. Other professionals may also request a copy of the energy report, such as a builder, contractor, or solar energy installer. Unless your report is emailed, provide others with photocopies of printed reports, and hold onto the original document.

Property Appraisal

The next step is obtaining a property appraisal, which the lender usually orders. In both the U.S. and Canada, the document format is substantially similar and called the *Uniform Residential Appraisal Report.*

The appraisal includes a comprehensive description of the home, property condition, a comparative market analysis, and photos. Most loans require an interior inspection of the property and photos. Depending upon the mortgage program, the lender may request an energy addendum, explained below.

Energy Addendum

An energy addendum is a written supplement to the real estate appraisal and is sometimes ordered by the builder in conjunction with obtaining a building certification such as LEED or Energy Star. The "Residential Green and Energy Efficient Addendum" was developed by the Appraisal Institute, the world's leading professional association of real estate appraisers.[176]

The energy addendum may be completed by any of the following people: builder, architect, contractor, certified green-building rater, home energy rater, energy consultant, solar energy installer, or a third-party verifier. More than one professional can take part in completing the report, and it must be provided to the appraiser prior to the appraisal inspection.

Real estate appraisers who have completed green-building and energy-efficient training may complete both the appraisal report and addendum. The following energy features are addressed in the addenda: insulation, building envelope, windows, lighting, skylights, Energy Star appliances, HVAC, water heating, indoor environmental quality, water efficiency, radon system, and utility costs. If applicable, the report includes specifications about solar photovoltaic panels, or pre-wired components for a "proposed solar installation."

Down Payment Assistance

Down payment assistance programs are available from government housing agencies, local partnerships, and nonprofits. Most incentives are aimed to assist first-time homebuyers and have income restrictions. However, local housing agencies are chartered to help their communities, and offer a broad range of programs, including programs without eligibility rules.

Funds are based on a percentage of the purchase price to help cover the down payment. As a rule, homebuyers must have a small cash investment, such as $1,500. Some incentives are increased to cover closing costs, repairs, and energy improvements. Because of the way programs are structured, any loan payments are usually not factored into the borrower qualification steps.

Types of Down Payment Assistance	
Zero-Interest Loans	Loans have no monthly payment. Most agencies offer 4 to 8% of purchase price, with additional incentives to cover the cost of energy improvements.
Amortizing Loans	Loans are long-term, at low- or very-low interest rates. Usually recorded as second mortgage. Loans 8 to 10% of purchase price cover down payment and closing costs. 20% of purchase price often available to cover energy improvements.
Forgivable Loans	Most often are zero interest with no monthly payments. At the end of each year, a certain percentage of the loan is forgiven. For example, $6,000 loan for 5-year term shrinks by about $1,200 each year as long as borrower continues living in the house.
Deferred Loans	Low-rate loans with no monthly payments for the first few years and not factored into loan qualifying ratios. Deferments are typically the first 3, 5, or 7 years, and payments are paid thereafter for about 20 years.
Soft Seconds	Also called "silent seconds." 25 to 30-year second lien at low- or very-low interest rate. Sometimes structured as a deferred payment loan. Many housing agency soft seconds are zero-interest loans.
Shared Equity	Can reduce or altogether eliminate the need for down payment funds. Homebuyers generally have maximum income requirements. Lender receives a specified percentage of equity when home is sold.

Canada Down Payment Assistance Program

The Government of Canada's *First-Time Home Buyer Incentive* is an initiative of the National Housing Strategy. The program offers first-time buyers 5 or 10% of the home's purchase price to put toward a down payment. Incentive is 10% for new construction and 5% for existing homes. Incentive is 5% for mobile and manufactured homes, either new or existing.[177]

The loan amount can be 4 times the qualifying income of borrower(s). For homes purchased in Toronto, Vancouver, or Victoria, the borrowing amount is increased to 4.5%. Homes purchased in the Census Metropolitan Areas of Toronto, Vancouver, or Victoria are eligible for qualifying income of $150,000.

The program is structured as a "shared equity" mortgage. This means that the government shares in the upside *and* downside of the property value. When the home is sold (or within a 25-year window), homeowners pay back the same percentage of the value of the home as initially borrowed, such as 5% or 10%. Below are two examples:

- *You receive $10,000 as a 5% incentive on a $200,000 home purchase. If the house is sold for $300,000, your payback would be 5% of $300,000 or $15,000.*
- *You receive $20,000 as a 10% incentive on a $200,000 home purchase. If the home value decreases to $150,000, your repayment would be 10% of the lower amount, or $15,000.*

Borrowers must meet the minimum down payment requirements with traditional funds such as savings or from a Registered Retirement Savings Plan (RRSP), or non-repayable financial gift from a relative or family member. The first mortgage must be greater than 80% of the property value and subject to a mortgage loan insurance premium, eligible through Canada Guaranty, CMHC, or Sagen.

Borrowers must be Canadian citizens, permanent residents, or non-permanent residents authorized to work in Canada. The incentive is available to first-time homebuyers, or those who have not occupied a home that you, your current spouse, or common-law partner owned in the last 4 years based. (*Note: refer to CHMC website guidelines for other circumstances).*[178]

Construction Loans

Construction loans, also known as "interim financing," are required when you are building your own home. Traditionally, such loans were limited to "custom-built" homes, involving an architect and professional builder. As long as the property meets the lender's underwriting guidelines for square footage and other features, there is financing available for the types of homes featured in Chapter 6, *Home Building Opportunities.* Outlined below are several construction-financing scenarios.

Custom Built Home

Often called "stick built," or "site built," the house is built on your own land by a local builder. If you also need a "land loan," your mortgage lender will explain if there are available options. Otherwise, the construction loan amount will only cover the cost of materials and labor for the house.

At closing, the lender will advance funds to the builder for the basement or foundation. Remaining funds are paid in several installments, as phases of work are completed and verified by an appraiser. If the loan will be converted to a "permanent mortgage," your lender may order an updated credit report and re-verify your income and financial assets.

Prefab, Log, Modular, or Manufactured Homes

The construction timeline for factory-built homes is short. Therefore, the mortgage process is often completed in one step. This type of loan is called a "single-close" or "construction-permanent" mortgage. Factory-built homes and prefabs are typically sold at two price levels:

Finished Cost
Often called "pre-built," the price includes land preparation, foundation, installation, permits, utility lines, and additional options, such as a deck or porch. This option offers the widest range of floor plans, exterior designs, and other features.

Base Cost
Often called "prefab kits," costs include delivery and a crew to assemble the house. Prior to delivery, you would arrange for the permits, utilities, land preparation, and foundation.

The most important step for homebuyers is to collect lots of paperwork, including cost estimates from builders, dealers, or manufacturers. Confirm every item that is included—and what's not included.

In order for a lender to explain what mortgage programs are available, they will need basic information such as construction type (e.g., modular, or stick-built), square footage, type of foundation, year-round heating, and other property details.

Land value is an important part of the equation for mortgage lenders. Provide the lot size and location of the building site, or a description of where you are seeking to purchase land and the expected cost.

Unless these steps are being handled by your builder or dealer, contact the local building department to obtain information regarding the cost and timeline of obtaining a building permit, and information regarding municipal water, private wells, septic systems, propane tanks, fireplaces, wood stoves, smoke detection, and so forth. Obtain information from utility companies regarding electricity and natural gas.

Chattel Financing

Technically, a chattel loan is a personal loan. Certain types of homes are considered personal property and not real estate, depending upon the type of foundation and other features. Mortgage lenders are required to make loans that reflect local zoning laws and property classifications.

The types of residential dwellings that require chattel financing include mobile homes on non-permanent foundations, moveable homes, houseboats, geodesic domes, shipping container homes, etc. Depending on the property size, foundation type, utilities, and year-round heating system, some tiny homes and accessory dwelling units (ADUs) can be classified as real estate.

National Mortgage Programs

The following pages outline energy-efficient mortgage programs that have been implemented by government-sponsored housing agencies in the United States and Canada.

Freddie Mac GreenCHOICE Mortgage

Homebuyers can apply for the *GreenCHOICE Mortgage* from any bank or mortgage lender that is authorized to sell loans to the Federal Home Loan Mortgage Corporation (Freddie Mac). Homebuyers can close on the mortgage prior to completion of improvements. Key features include:

- Improvements can be up to 15% of the as-completed value
- Basic energy-efficient improvements with aggregate cost of $6,500 or less do not require an energy report.
- Energy-efficient features to be financed can include:
    - Solar panels and photovoltaic systems
    - Solar hot water systems
    - Ceiling, wall, or floor insulation
    - Low-flow water fixtures
    - Energy-efficient windows and doors
    - High-performance HVAC
    - Weatherization and air sealing
    - Energy-saving appliances
    - Programmable thermostats

Manufactured homes are eligible, as long as the energy-efficiency improvements do not impact the structural integrity of the property. GreenCHOICE mortgages are available on Freddie Mac fixed-rate and adjustable mortgage programs for purchase and no cash-out refinances. The down payment is 3% for borrowers eligible for Freddie Mac *Home Possible* purchase transactions.[179]

Freddie Mac — Affordable Seconds

Borrowers in need of down payment assistance are eligible to have a subordinate lien in conjunction with the *Home Possible* first mortgage program. A subordinate lien can be structured as a "soft second," or "shared equity" agreement. Funds must be provided by a governmental housing agency or other authorized entity or non-profit.[180]

Fannie Mae HomeStyle Energy Mortgage

Homebuyers can apply for a Fannie Mae *HomeStyle Energy Mortgage* from any bank or mortgage lender authorized to sell loans to the Federal National Mortgage Association (Fannie Mae). Homebuyers can close on the mortgage prior to completion of improvements.[181] Key features include:

- Improvements can be up to 15% of the as-completed value
- Down payment of as little as 3% based on loan transaction
- Debt-to-income ratio (DTI) may be expanded based on the home energy score (if other DTI requirements are not met)
- Available on primary residence, second homes, and investment properties
- Available on 1-4 family residences and manufactured homes
- No minimum for the cost of energy improvements
- Borrowers must obtain a home energy report to identify recommended improvements and estimated cost savings
- No energy report is required for:
    - Basic weatherization and water efficient items up to $3,500
    - Solar panels
    - Wind power devices
    - Geothermal systems
    - Other renewable energy sources
    - Environmental hazard damage repairs
    - Radon mitigation

Fannie Mae — Community Seconds

Borrowers in need of down payment assistance are eligible to have a subordinate lien in conjunction with affordable programs such as *HomeReady*. A subordinate liens can be structured as an amortizing loan with level monthly payments, and other types such as deferred payments or a forgivable loan. Funds must be provided by a governmental agency or authorized entity.[182]

FHA Energy Efficient Mortgage

Homebuyers can apply for the Federal Housing Administration (FHA) Energy Efficient Mortgage from any mortgage lender that is authorized to originate FHA-insured mortgages.

FHA allows the debt-to-income ratio to stretch by 2 points due to the savings resulting from the energy improvements. The program is available on both purchase and refinance transactions on primary-residence properties. A home energy assessment is required unless $3,500 or less is needed for basic weatherization. The minimum down payment is 3.5% based on the as-completed value (referred to as *adjusted value* by the FHA).

There are two methods for determining how much can be financed with the mortgage to cover the cost of energy improvements. The FHA rule is to add the "lesser of" either the cost-effective improvements noted on the energy rater's report (or) the "lesser of" 5% for any of the following:[183]

- Adjusted property value
- 115% of the current median area price of a 1-family home
- 150% of the current national conforming mortgage limit.

The chart below is a simplified version of the above rule, and figures do not reflect actual home values or loan limits.

The lowest number shown can be financed ↓			
Cost-effective improvements noted on energy report	$ 12,000		$ 12,000
Adjusted property value	$ 220,000	x 5%	$ 11,000
115% of median area price	$ 330,000	x 5%	$ 16,500
150% of national loan limits	$ 450,000	x 5%	$ 22,500

Under FHA's *Solar and Wind Technologies* policy, borrowers can have a higher mortgage amount in order to pay for the cost and installation of a new solar or wind energy system on a home purchase or refinance.[184]

VA Energy Efficient Mortgage

Eligible veterans, active military servicemembers, and qualified spouses can obtain an energy-efficient mortgage from any mortgage lender approved by the U.S. Department of Veterans Affairs. Homebuyers can apply from any mortgage lender that is authorized to originate VA-insured mortgages.

Loans are available for purchase transactions or refinancing. Acceptable improvements include, but are not limited to, heating, cooling, and water systems; insulation; storm windows and doors; weatherproofing; heat pumps; furnace upgrades; and renewable energy systems. Lenders must evaluate whether proposed improvements are reasonable for the home in question.

Improvements of $3,000 or less do not require an energy report; however, the lender will request an itemization of energy measures, along with costs. With an energy report, borrowers can obtain up to $6,000. For improvements that cost $6,000 or more, an energy report is required. If the projected savings in utility costs is equal to—or less—than the increase in housing payment, financing is generally acceptable.

USDA Rural Energy Plus

Homebuyers can submit a loan application with any mortgage lender that is authorized to originate USDA Rural Housing mortgages under the Rural Housing Services agency of the U.S. Department of Agriculture (USDA). Loans are available to low- and moderate-income borrowers to build or buy a home located in designated rural areas. Loan eligibility is based on property location, household income, and the number of people in the household.

The USDA Rural Energy Plus loan allows homebuyers to purchase a home with a zero-down payment for homes that meet the International Energy Conservation Code (IECC) standards. Homes can be a new construction that was built to a comparable code, or an existing home. Loan qualification is expanded due to potential savings in utility costs.

The USDA *Property and Income Eligibility* online tool is available to the public. Using the flash map, you can drop a pin on any location to explore opportunities. The site includes helpful tools and loan eligibility calculators.

Canada Mortgage and Housing — Green Home

Canada Mortgage and Housing Corporation (CMHC) offers the Green Home incentive program that is available to homebuyers who are making energy-efficient home improvements. The program is also available to borrowers who buy, build, or renovate a home using CMHC-insured financing.

Incentives are in the form of a mortgage insurance refund and structured in accordance with building standards and energy ratings. To qualify, homes must be assessed by a qualified Natural Resources Canada (NRCan) energy advisor *before and after* the energy improvements are made. Below is a chart listing the refund standards.[185]

Homes built under the following building standards are automatically eligible for a partial loan insurance refund		
25% PREMIUM REFUND:	R-2000	
15% PREMIUM REFUND: ▪ Built Green (National) ▪ Energy Star (National) ▪ LEED Canada for Homes (National) ▪ GreenHouse (ON) ▪ GreenHome (YK) ▪ Novoclimat (QC) ▪ Manitoba Hydro's New Homes Program (MB)		
Homes NOT built under an eligible building standard must be assessed by NRCan Qualified Energy Advisor, which complies with the following:		
	15% REFUND	25% REFUND
EnerGuide Rating 0-100 Scale	Rating 82 – 85	Rating 86 – 100
EnerGuide Rating Gigajoules per year scale	Rating at least 15% lower than a typical new house	Rating at least 40% lower than a typical new house

Information source: Canada Mortgage and Housing Corporation

Canada Guaranty Energy-Efficient Advantage Program

The Canada Guaranty *Energy-Efficient Advantage Program* rewards borrowers who purchase or renovate a home with energy-efficient upgrades. Through the *Energy-Efficient Advantage Program*, qualified homebuyers may be eligible to receive a partial premium refund of up to 25%.

The program is available on new or existing homes built under one of Canada's energy-efficient building programs. Eligible properties coincide with the 15% to 25% standards for the CMHC Green Home Program, outlined on the previous page.

Homes not built under a qualified program are also eligible under the same CMHC standards. Key program features are summarized below.[186]

- Applicable to all Canada Guaranty mortgage insurance products.
- Purchase: new construction or existing home.
- Purchase with improvements for energy-efficiency purposes.
- Mortgage financing must be insured through Canada Guaranty.
- Canada Guaranty must receive all original mortgage insurance premiums and applicable fees prior to issuing the partial premium refund.
- Partial premium refund applications must be submitted within 24 months of the mortgage closing date.
- Renovations of existing homes qualify for 15 to 25% refunds based on EnerGuide rating on 0–100 scale structured according to pre- and post-improvement ratings.
- Condominium units purchased in high-rise buildings built to the LEED Canada New Construction standard (Certified Silver, Gold, and Platinum) automatically qualify for a 15% premium refund. Buildings that are 40% more energy-efficient than compliance with applicable building codes are eligible for a 25% refund.

Property Assessed Clean Energy (PACE) Financing Available in U.S. and Canada

"Property Assessed Clean Energy" (PACE) is an innovative financing program that enables residential homeowners to borrow funds for energy improvements that are permanently affixed to the property. Instead of paying a bank or mortgage lender, loans are repaid with the homeowner's property tax bill. PACE financing can cover 100% of the improvements, and generally loans are for 20-year terms.

Although PACE is a national initiative, programs are established on a local level. Each state or province can adopt the PACE program as legislature or a provincial economic development initiative. Local municipalities (city, town, or county) can then develop a PACE financing program that aligns with the local needs of the community. Nonprofit corporations may serve as an intermediary administrator of a PACE program. Local authorizations can be made available to nonprofits, commercial businesses, or residential homeowners.

If you decide to sell your home, some programs are structured to allow the loan to be transferred to a person who buys your home. There are mortgage refinancing programs, however, that do require PACE loans to be paid off with the new mortgage. This is because tax assessments are "priority liens," which subordinate the claim position of a first mortgage, as well as other liens such as a second mortgage or home equity line of credit.

(Note: Chapter 10, Rebates and Incentives, denotes whether PACE financing has been approved by legislation for each state and province.)

Mortgage Affordability Chart						
GROSS ANNUAL INCOME ↓	**← Monthly Payments for Recurring Debts →**					*Monthly Escrows*
	0	**200**	**400**	**600**	**800**	
30,000	160,000	120,000	80,000	40,000	0	*200*
40,000	220,000	180,000	140,000	100,000	60,000	*200*
50,000	260,000	220,000	180,000	140,000	100,000	*300*
60,000	340,000	300,000	260,000	220,000	180,000	*300*
70,000	380,000	340,000	300,000	260,000	220,000	*400*
80,000	440,000	400,000	360,000	320,000	280,000	*400*
90,000	500,000	460,000	420,000	380,000	340,000	*500*
100,000	560,000	520,000	480,000	440,000	400,000	*500*
110,000	620,000	580,000	540,000	500,000	460,000	*500*
120,000	700,000	660,000	620,000	580,000	540,000	*500*

Estimates based on 40% DTI ratio; 30-year mortgage at 4.375% interest; monthly escrows for real estate property tax, hazard insurance, and FHA or PMI insurance for 90% LTV.

The above chart is a very broad and conservative estimate for loan affordability. Locate your gross annual income (for all borrowers). From left to right, choose a column that is closest to your "recurring debts," such as car loans and 5% of credit card balances. The intersection of these two points indicates an approximate mortgage. For example:

$60,000 income and $400 debt = $260,000 mortgage

The monthly escrows shown in the far-right column are factored into the maximum loan amount. For example: $300 covers $150 for property taxes, $75 for hazard insurance, and $75 for FHA or PMI mortgage insurance.

Loan qualification typically requires that the housing payment will not exceed 30% of gross monthly income; and all monthly debts—including the housing payment—do not exceed 40% of income. Some of the mortgage programs featured in this chapter allow debt ratios as high as 45%.

Qualifying ratios can be specific to factors such as the loan-to-value, credit score, occupancy, loan purpose, and liquid assets available after the closing. Loan payments with fewer than 10 months remaining are excluded. Credit card debt is based on the combined current balances of all cards. For example: $10,000 x 5% = $500.

How to Compute the Debt-to-Income Ratio (DTI)

Loan Payments	Total of monthly loan payments →	$
Credit Cards	5% of total balance owed →	$
HOUSING PAYMENT	Estimated PITI amount →	$
TOTAL DEBTS	Total of above items →	$ (A)
INCOME	Gross Monthly Income →	$ (B)
DTI RATIO	Divide total debt (A) by income (B)	%

How to Compute the Housing Payment Ratio and Debt-to-Income Ratio

Loan Payments	Total of monthly loan payments →	$
Credit Cards	5% of total balance owed →	$
HOUSING PAYMENT	Estimated PITI amount →	$ (A)
TOTAL DEBTS	Total of above items →	$ (B)
INCOME	Gross Monthly Income →	$ (C)
PAYMENT RATIO	Divide payment (A) by income (C)	%
DTI RATIO	Divide total debt (B) by income (C)	%

Resources

Freddie Mac GreenCHOICE Mortgage
https://sf.freddiemac.com/working-with-us/origination-underwriting/mortgage-products/greenchoice-mortgages

Fannie Mae HomeStyle Energy
https://singlefamily.fanniemae.com/originating-underwriting/mortgage-products/homestyle-energy-mortgage

FHA Energy-Efficient Mortgage
https://www.hud.gov/program_offices/housing/sfh/eem/energy-r

VA Energy Efficient Mortgage
https://www.va.gov/housing-assistance/home-loans/loan-types/

USDA Rural Housing, Income and Property Eligibility Site
https://eligibility.sc.egov.usda.gov/eligibility/welcomeAction.do

Canada First Time Homebuyer Incentive
https://www.placetocallhome.ca/fthbi/first-time-homebuyer-incentive

Canada Mortgage and Housing Green Home
https://www.cmhc-schl.gc.ca/en/consumers/home-buying/mortgage-loan-insurance-for-consumers/cmhc-green-home

Canada Guaranty Energy-Efficient Advantage
https://www.canadaguaranty.ca/energy-efficient-advantage-program/

PACE Nation
https://www.pacenation.org/pace-programs/

Housing Finance 2020
New Mortgages for the New Generation of Homebuyers
https://annadesimone.net

CHAPTER 9

Financial Payback and True Cost of Home Ownership

A RETURN ON YOUR INVESTMENT IS A FORM OF PAYBACK. Your home is a wealth-building asset, and probably the largest financial investment in your lifetime. Real estate growth is called "appreciation," and as long as market conditions in your area are favorable, your property value will continue to increase. Based on a modest growth rate of 5% per year, the value of a home purchased for $200,000 will more than double in 15 years. If you take good care of your house, this increase in value can effectively serve as a safe and secure retirement account.

Growth in Real Estate (5% per year)

The chart on the previous page shows property value increases in 5-year increments. The actual dollars that would go into your pocket if you sold your home is known as "equity." To calculate equity, subtract the outstanding mortgage balance from the property value.

The chart below is based on the same house, but with an added layer—the mortgage. This scenario assumes a zero-down payment. If the house were sold for in 20 years for $530,600, the remaining mortgage balance of $93,700 would be paid. The owner would receive $436,900 in cash.

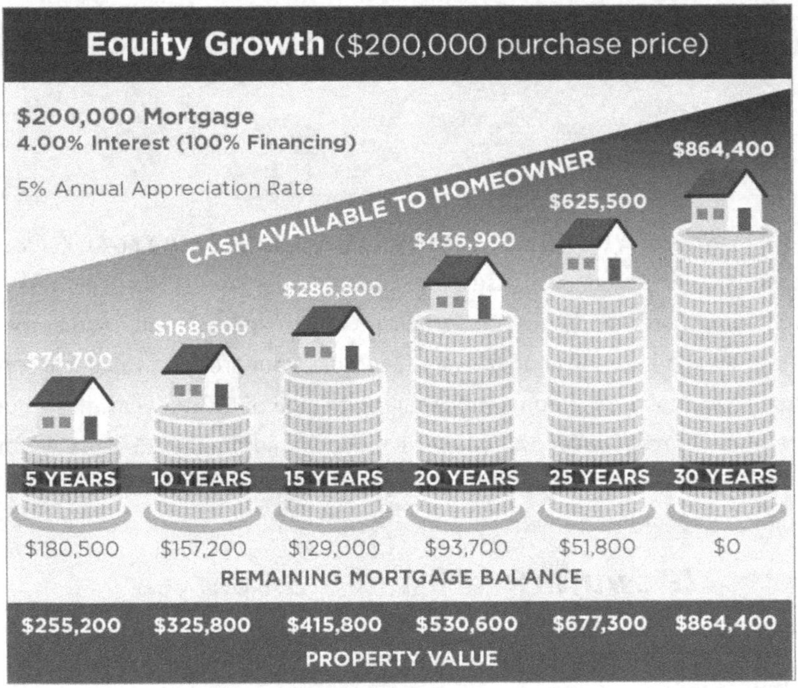

Even if you have no plans to sell your home, it's always good to know how much equity you have available. If cash is needed for any reason, it can be accessed through refinancing the mortgage or taking out a home equity line of credit.

Figures in both charts are based on an annual appreciation rate of 5%, which is considered a conservative industry standard. Figures are rounded to nearest $100. Recent market conditions for the United States and Canada are discussed in the next topic.

U.S. and Canada Real Estate Markets

As of October 2020, the nationwide average of home prices in the United States increased 7.3% year-over-year, according to the CoreLogic Home Price Index (HPI) report.[187]

The real estate marketplace, Zillow, stated in its November 2020 article, *Home Values Rising Faster than at Any Time Since 2005*, "Metropolitan areas such as Seattle, Washington, Phoenix, Arizona, and San Jose, California saw increases in the 12 to 13% range. Dozens of other metropolitan areas across the U.S. reported increases greater than 7%."[188]

Global Property Guide's January 2021 article, *Canada's Red Hot Housing Market*, reported that house prices in Canada's 11 major cities rose by 9.36% during 2020. This represents the 12th straight year of home price growth. The article also reported that, based on figures from the Canadian Real Estate Association, for the last quarter of 2020 homes across Canada increased in value by 15.9% for 1-story single family homes, and rose 16.5% for 2-story single-family homes.[189]

Property Values of Energy-Efficient Homes

A study completed by the Federal Home Loan Mortgage Corporation (Freddie Mac), concluded that energy-efficient homes sell for higher prices. The study, *Energy Efficiency: Value Added to Properties and Loan Performance,* released October 2019, revealed that homes with higher energy assessment ratings sold for 3 to 5% more than homes with lower ratings.

The study examined existing homes rated by the Residential Energy Services Network (RESNET) HERS rating system, and new construction homes rated with the Department of Energy's Home Energy Score. The study also showed that energy-efficient homes had a lower delinquency rate than unrated homes.[190]

As stated earlier in Chapter 1, a study completed by the North Carolina Building Performance Association revealed that homes with green certification programs such as Energy Star sold for 9.5% more than non-certified homes.[191]

In its *Market Impact Study*, the North Carolina Energy Efficiency Alliance reported that Energy Star homes were found to have a statistically significant market advantage compared to similar code-built homes. Homes sold almost three months faster than average, and for a significantly higher sales price and higher prices per square-foot than code-built homes.[192]

> **In addition to higher re-sale value, Energy Star homes sell 89 days faster than traditional homes.**
>
> — North Carolina Energy Efficiency Alliance

The world-renown environmental nonprofit, Rocky Mountain Institute (RMI), completed a study, *The Economics of Zero-Energy Homes—Single-Family Insights*, that analyzed zero energy homes in four locations across the nation. The study concluded that, on average, zero energy homes cost 7.3% more to build than a code-built home. Zero energy ready homes averaged 1.8% in added costs. Payback periods for the added energy costs ranged from 7.8 to 13.8 years, according to the RMI study. Payback will vary depending upon several factors: local costs, climate, and building codes.[193]

Efficiency Vermont examined three residential building types in its *Net Zero Energy Feasibility Study.* The study compared the cost of ownership of zero energy residences compared to a similar code-built homes. The study concluded that net zero homes were a better investment, even before re-bates or incentives.[194]

Berkeley National Laboratory's report, *Selling into the Sun: Price Premium Analysis of a Multi-State Dataset of Solar Homes*, concluded that homes in with solar photovoltaic (PV) panels in some areas sold for more money than homes without panels. The study analyzed sales of more than 20,000 homes in 7 states, representing homes with and without PV panels. All homes in the study sold for less than $900,000. The study concluded that homebuyers consistently were willing to pay more for a property with PV panels across a variety of states, and at an average market premium of about $15,000.[195]

Berkeley National Laboratory's Environmental Energy Technologies Division completed a study entitled *"A Meta-Analysis of Single-Family Deep Energy Retrofit Performance in the U.S."* The study analyzed deep energy retrofit projects on 116 homes located across the nation, and with an average cost of $40,000. Based on the assumption that costs were financed for a 30-year term, the study concluded that the increase in mortgage costs was balanced out by the savings in energy costs.[196]

Sustainable Buildings Are Value-Added

SEEFAR Building Analytics Inc., based in Winnipeg, Manitoba, developed the SEEFAR-Valuation® life-cycle cost assessment tool which defines a home's sustainability and energy efficiency in dollars and cents. The tool supplements energy rating systems and evaluates the "true cost of home ownership." SEEFAR's value-added approach goes "beyond visible value."

The process for accurately calculating the value-added for a building is based on a life-cycle analysis known as the Total Cost of Building Ownership (TCBO). TCBO projects operating and maintenance costs over and above the purchase price that occur after construction is completed. Accumulated costs include mortgage interest, property taxes, hazard insurance, energy costs, and maintenance and renewal (M&R).[197]

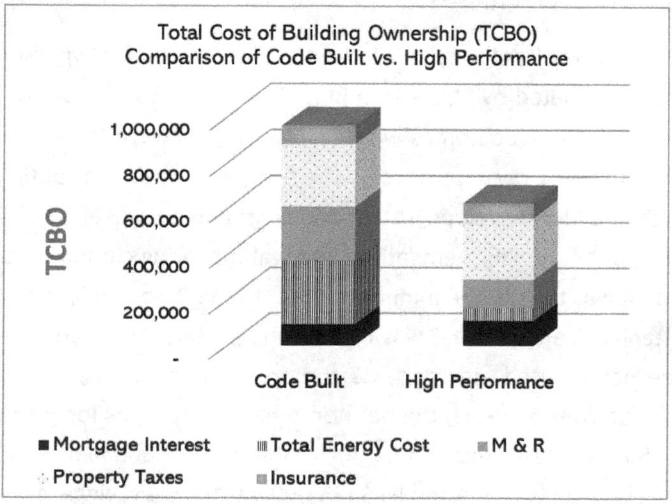

© SEEFAR Building Analytics Inc.

In the above example, the M&R (and cost escalation due to inflation) for the high-performance home is $336,000, or 35% less for the code-built home. SEEFAR-Valuations are often used by lenders and appraisers to show "dollar value" of high-performance homes, and that value extends to the buyer when the house is sold.

Jim Nostedt, P. Eng. of SEEFAR explains the TCBO concept: "Although homeowners stay in a home an average of 12 years, the useful life of a home is 60 years—before major retrofit might be required. Building a high-performance home may cost a little more upfront (3 to 10%) but reduces the TCBO by 30 to 40%."

TCBO and Equity	Home A	Home B	Home C
Mortgage Interest	$110,730	$118,523	$119,002
Annual Service & Maint.	54,200	43,653	37,989
Building Renewal	131,897	141,646	127,560
Energy Costs	422,255	209,264	99,250
Property Taxes	362,368	365,252	370,129
Insurance Costs	110,286	111,806	111,806
Net Home Equity	642,128	813,417	813,417
Net Home Ownership Cost	$549,709	$277,097	$52,319

© SEEFAR Building Analytics, Inc

The TCBO & Equity chart above indicates the "Net Home Ownership Cost" in a study completed by SEEFAR on behalf of Manitoba Hydro. The design and layout of the three homes were similar, and all were located in Manitoba. SEEFAR noted key differences in the energy construction configuration, such as the building envelope insulation levels, and energy-efficiency differences in heating, cooling, ventilation, and water heating components.

Home A was built to the minimum code, Home B was built to the *Power Smart* standard, and Home C was built to the passive low energy standard. All three homes used electricity as the sole energy source. The analysis showed that, over 60 years, the net home ownership costs for Home C was nearly $500,000 less than Home A, saving about $600 per month. Importantly, net equity is boosted by $323,000 due to 76% savings in energy.[198]

Quantifying Payback

As explained throughout this chapter, the true cost of home ownership is lower for energy-efficient homes. In addition to higher resale values and lower costs for energy and maintenance, there are a few other financial considerations that further reduce overall costs:

- *Higher mortgage loan amounts due to expanded underwriting rules for energy-efficient homes.*
- *Ability to purchase a home with less cash, shortening the years spent saving money, and buying before prices get any higher.*
- *Greater increase in property value and in building home equity.*
- *Bottom-line income tax credits for installing renewable energy.*
- *Income tax deductions for certain energy improvements.*
- *Cash rebates on thousands of appliances and other purchases.*
- *Affordable energy improvement loans from municipal and housing partnership agencies, utility companies, and lenders.*

Quality of Life Payback

The kind of payback that cannot be mathematically quantified includes a healthy home and your quality of life. It is vital that your home fits your lifestyle and priorities. Location has historically been a strong focus in the real estate industry, but it's hard to be happy in a new home if you're not happy where you live.

If you're seeking "walkability," and love the urban vibe, you will be happier if you find a home near a city. Remember, riding a bicycle to work and using public transportation also lower your carbon footprint.

If you are longing to have a backyard garden to grow your own organic vegetables, or have lots of room for your children and pets to play, then you will be happier when you find a home with some extra land.

When making your final decision for buying a new home, keep in mind that ultimate payback is your happiness. Sometimes that means the town where you grew up in is ***simply the place you're meant to be.***

Helping Homebuyers Make Informed Decisions

by Sam Rashkin

As Chief Architect in the Building Technologies Office in the U.S. Department of Energy, Sam earned a national reputation for his work in developing the Energy Star Certified Home Program, and the Zero Energy Ready Home.

We are living in the age of the informed homebuyer. Across the board consumer purchases from dining to car-buying have been transformed with greater buyer information. This includes a vast amount of online data and peer reviews that effectively screen out non-competitive options, and help increase confidence in smart purchase decisions.

A new software application has just been developed for buying homes—the ultimate consumer product.

There are effectively two price tags for every home. However, only one—the advertised price—is presented to consumers. The second, the hidden maintenance liability, is a huge fear and unknown for homebuyers. In fact, this was reported by Zillow in the article, *Unexpected Repairs and Maintenance Top the List of Regrets for Homeowners.*[199]

Zillow's survey noted that 36% of homeowners expressed regret at dealing with unexpected repairs and maintenance. And these hidden costs often require substantial expenses beyond those for mortgage, taxes and insurance payments that push so many homeowners to their financial limits.

The first step to helping homebuyers make informed decisions is to reveal the critically important home maintenance price tag to homebuyers for each home under consideration.

Information about TruHome Facts™ is provided on the next page.
http://www.truhomefacts.com/

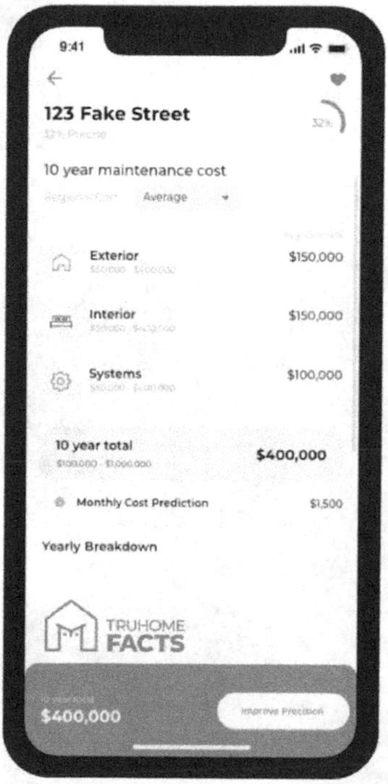

TruHome Facts™

Simply enter an address to access information about any property for free.

Quickly projects maintenance costs for the next 10 years for exterior, interior, and systems, and specific upgrades and repairs for each year.

Sam was recognized for his contributions to sustainable housing with the prestigious Hanley Award in 2012 and EEBA Legend Award in 2019. During his 20-plus years as a licensed architect, Sam specialized in energy-efficient design and completed over 100 high-performance residential projects. He has served on national Steering Committees for USGBC's LEED for Homes, NAHB's Green Builder Guidelines, EPA's Water Sense label, and EPA's Indoor airPLUS label. Sam has also prepared hundreds of articles, technical papers, reports, and seminars, and has contributed to other books on energy-efficient and green construction.

Sam's newest book titled "Housing 2.0: Home is Where Life Happens" is a unique guide for optimizing the housing user experience. Sam now engages the housing industry on applying the wide range of strategies and best practices from the book that can result in 30 to 70% savings and added value per home.

CHAPTER 10

Rebates and Incentives
by State & Province

ENERGY INITIATIVES BY CANADIAN PROVINCE

ALBERTA

- Banff offers various incentives including solar energy production.
- Canmore offers solar energy rebates.
- *Clean Energy Improvement Program* for residential property owners. Up to 100% financing of project costs.
- Edmonton *Change Homes for Climate* solar program offers solar energy incentives.
- Energy Efficiency Alberta offers rebates on retrofit projects such as heat recovery systems.
- Lethbridge offers various energy-efficiency incentives.
- Medicine Hat offers the *HAT Smart Program*.
- PACE financing approved by provincial government. Loan programs are established by municipality.

BRITISH COLUMBIA

- BC Energy *Step Code* program offers incentives for new energy efficient homes built to beat the BC code.
- BC Hydro offers home renovation rebate, *Power Smart* program for low-income households, and upgrade assistance to non-profit and Aboriginal housing.
- *Better Homes* and *Home Renovation Rebate* programs offered through Clean BC, BC Hydro, and FortisBC.
- City of Nelson offers the *EcoSave* energy retrofits program.
- Efficiency BC offers a home renovation rebate and efficiency program.
- Fortis BC offers numerous rebate programs for various types of heat pumps, insulation, hot water heaters, furnaces, boilers, *EnerChoice* fireplaces. Assistance programs for energy conservation, home renovation, and new home construction.
- FortisBC, BC Hydro, and municipalities are offering free energy savings kits to income-qualified BC residents. Kit include LED lighting and other energy-saving items.
- Fortis BC, BC Hydro offers the following incentives to income-qualified residents: rebates on natural gas furnaces, boilers, and water heaters; free installation on other energy saving equipment; and free coaching on how to save energy at home.
- Kamloops *See the Heat* program lets residents borrow a thermal imaging camera free of charge, along with a draft proofing kit for windows, doors, and electrical switches.
- PACE financing approved by provincial government. Loan programs are established by municipality.
- PST tax exemption for alternative energy generation and conservation equipment, including insulation, weather stripping, solar PV, micro-hydro and more.
- RDN Grade *Site-cut Timber Program* home construction and renovation incentives in the districts of Nanaimo and Lantzville. Other incentives for solar PV/thermal, and geothermal energy systems.
- Vancouver *Heritage Energy Retrofit* program offered through the Vancouver Heritage Foundation for homes built before 140 on listed on the historic register.

MANITOBA

- Efficiency Manitoba First Nations program provides free insulation, LED lighting, and other energy saving items.
- Efficiency Manitoba offers a full range of rebates and financing incentives under their *New Home Program*, plus retrofit and upgrade incentives for heat recovery ventilators (HRV) controls, roof upgrade, home insulation, doors, and windows.
- Efficiency Manitoba offers energy upgrade programs for income-qualified and Indigenous households. Free and subsidized energy efficiency upgrades for income-qualifying households in partnership with Metis.
- Green energy equipment tax credits are offered by the Government of Manitoba for geothermal heat pump or solar energy systems.
- Manitoba Hydro offers on-bill financing for upgrades to gas and electrical systems; *Pay As You Save (PAYS)* financing program; home energy efficiency loans; residential *Earth Power* loans for cold climate air-source heat pumps, geothermal heat pumps, solar hot water heaters.

NEW BRUNSWICK

- *Community Outreach Program* provides energy-savings kits and training for not-for-profit organizations. Kits include LED lightbulbs, water-efficient showerheads, faucet aerators and water heater pipe wrap.
- NB Power offers cash incentives for homes that exceed the national building code.
- NB Power offers the *Total Home Energy Savings* money-back program for efficiency upgrades for insulation, air-sealing, HVAC, windows, doors, and more. Programs for low-income homeowners.

NEWFOUNDLAND AND LABRADOR

- Newfoundland Power and Newfoundland and Labrador Hydro offer the *takeCHARGE* Energy-Efficient Loan Program (EELP) to subsidize financing required to purchase and install a qualified heat pump, insulation, and/or home energy assessments through monthly payments on customer's electricity bill. Thermostat rebate program offered through *takeCHARGE*.

- Newfoundland and Labrador Housing offer the *Home Energy Savings Program (HESP),* a provincial initiative for energy retrofits for low-income households.

NORTHWEST TERRITORIES

- Artic Energy Alliance offers heat recovery rebates to homeowners of older, less energy-efficient homes in the Northwest Territories (NWT) to reduce costs and greenhouse gas emissions associated with heating their homes.
- Artic Energy Alliance offers funding for renewable energy sources such as solar, wind, wood pellet heating, biofuel/synthetic gas, and ground source heat pumps; this funding is available to non-profit organizations, businesses, and community governments.

NOVA SCOTIA

- Efficiency Nova Scotia offers financial incentives for the purchase of solar photovoltaic systems.
- Efficiency Nova Scotia offers heating system rebates, appliance retirement, home warming, and a free home energy assessment program. Free home efficiency upgrades such as insulation and air sealing are available to income-qualified residents.
- Efficiency Nova Scotia offers rebates for new construction energy efficient homes.
- Efficiency Nova Scotia offers rebates, incentives, financing, and expert advice for energy-efficient upgrades, and no-cost installation through qualified partners for certain products.
- Government of Nova Scotia offers *Your Energy Rebate*. For most participants, rebates are automatically taken off the power company bill for home-delivered oil, propane, and natural gas. Other sources such as firewood and wood pellet can apply for rebate.

NUNAVUT

- Nunavut Housing Corporation provides the *Home Renovation Program*, offering financial and technical assistance to homeowners who wish to carryout major repairs, renovations, and additions to their home. Programs also available for energy efficiency improvements.

ONTARIO

- Enbridge Gas, Inc. offers an energy-efficiency rebate program for home renovations; an affordable housing program for energy retrofits; a custom solutions and incentives program to help customers implement energy; incentives for purchase and installation of air curtain to prevent outside air from entering inside areas; incentives for HVAC; kitchen ventilation; ventilation; recovery ventilators; energy-recovery ventilators; smart thermostats.
- Genworth Financial Canada offers the *Energy-efficient Housing Program* for homebuyers purchasing an energy-efficient home such as the R-2000 and Energy Star.
- Hydro One offers the *First Nations Conservation Program* for energy-efficient upgrades at zero cost and no installation charges to residents in eligible communities.
- PACE financing is approved by provincial government. Loan programs are established by municipality.
- *Save On Energy* home assistance program for qualified Ontario homeowners.
- Toronto offers the *Home Energy Loan Program (HELP)*, low-interest loans for energy and water efficiency for homeowners. City provides funding for cost of improvements, and homeowners repay over time through installments on their property tax bill.
- Union Gas Limited offers incentives for space heating, energy recovery, and heat recovery ventilators.

PRINCE EDWARD ISLAND

- Efficiency PEI offers a building envelope upgrade rebate; rebates for installation of Energy Star certified heating equipment, water saving devices, biomass heating devices and other products.
- Efficiency PEI will subsidize the cost of an EnerGuide home evaluation, and further subsidize costs if homeowners choose to proceed with efficiency upgrades.
- The *New Home Construction Program* includes a review of building plans by a certified energy advisor; rebates on EnerGuide assessments.

- The *Winter Warming* program provides free air sealing and energy-efficient upgrades to qualified low to moderate-income residents. An efficiency PEI tradesperson completes tasks free of charge. Vouchers available for a free heating system cleaning and other efficiency products.

QUEBÉC

- Énergir offers incentives for adopting an energy-wise lifestyle. Low-income household supplement provides financial assistance. Rebates for programmable electronic thermostats.
- Énergir offers the *Combo System Grant* for purchase and installation of tankless water heater combined with a fan coil unit. High-efficiency water heater grants are available to cover the costs of a high-efficiency direct contact water heater. Retrofit rebates are available for the purchase of a natural gas boiler or converting an oil-fired system to a new natural gas system.
- Énergir offers the *Superior Energy-Efficiency Boiler* financial incentive by paying the cost difference between high-performance units and basic models. The *Tankless Water Heater Grant* offers $250 toward the purchase of a high-efficiency tankless water heater.
- Gazifére offers homeowners financial support for the purpose of an air exchange equipped with a heat recovery system, condensing water heater programs, tankless water heaters, and smart thermostats.
- Gouvernement du Québec offers the *Chauffez Vert* program for replacement of fossil-fueled systems with a renewable source for heating or water heater.
- The Novoclimat Homes program promotes construction of new high energy performance homes; the *Réoclimat* program is an energy renovation program for single-family homes, semi-detached homes, or row houses. Program includes energy audit before and after the retrofit, and access to financial assistance to carry out insulation work, upgrades to HVAC, installation of geothermal, and other incentives.
- Hydro Québec offers the *Energy Efficiency Retrofit* program for low-income households to install Energy Star certified windows, patio doors, insulation, and heat recovery ventilation.

- Transition Énergétique Québec offers rebates and other incentives to such as insulation, air sealing, windows, doors, water heating systems, and geothermal systems; other rebates for heat pumps and heating systems; other incentives and free items are available to income-qualified households.
- Transition Énergétique Québec offers rebates for newly built energy-efficient homes.

SASKATCHEWAN

- SaskPower and SaskEnergy have implemented a full range of programs to commercial and business to support energy efficiency. Programs include the *Commercial Boiler Program, Commercial Space and Water Heating Rebate* for Energy Star certified products.
- SaskPower business programs include the *Demand Response* program, the *Industrial Energy Optimization Program*, and the *Walk-through Assessment Program.*
- Saskatchewan Environmental Society is a province-wide K through 12 action campaign that promotes energy conservation all school year.

YUKON

- Government of Yukon, Energy, Mines and Resources promotes energy-efficient upgrades in commercial and institutional buildings.
- The *Good Energy Program* is a rebate program offered by the Yukon Government through the Energy Solutions Centre to encourage energy-efficient decisions in purchasing household appliances, products, services and heating systems. incentives for appliances, heating systems, and water conservation is a Yukon Government program offering rebates towards the purchase of Energy Star certified appliances.

Energy Initiatives by U.S. State

ALABAMA

POLICY

- PACE financing approved by state legislation. Loan programs are established by municipality.
- Property tax exemption for qualifying renewable energy installation.
- Sales tax exemption for purchase of qualified renewable energy systems.
- State income tax deduction of 100% of cost to convert from gas or electricity to a wood-burning system if wood is primary heating source for home.

INCENTIVES

- Alabama Power Company
- Central Alabama Electric Cooperative
- Dixie Electric Cooperative Wiregrass Electric Cooperative

ALASKA

POLICY

- Alaska solar easement law allows parties to voluntarily enter into solar easement contracts to ensure adequate sun exposure.
- Net metering permitted for all renewable energy sources. Excess generation credited to next bill at non-firm rate; carries over indefinitely.
- Property tax exemption for installed renewable energy systems.

INCENTIVES

- Alaska Housing Finance Corporation (AHFC)
- Golden Valley Electrical Association's *SNAP Program*

ARIZONA

POLICY

- City of Tucson requires all new construction for single family homes and duplexes built as solar-ready and able to accommodate solar water heating and photovoltaics for installation at a future date.

- Homeowners' associations (HOA) may not prohibit installation of solar energy panels and devices.
- Maricopa County Zoning Ordinance contains provisions for siting renewable energy systems for residential properties.
- Net metering permitted for all renewable energy systems. Various polices for net billing.
- Personal tax credit for renewable energy production; available on solar thermal, solar PV, wind, biomass, and landfill gas.
- Pima County has specific solar and wind permitting standards.
- Property tax assessment incentive for solar, wind, hydro energy.
- Solar and wind access by Arizona law protects individual homeowners' private property rights to solar access.
- Solar and wind equipment sales tax exemption.
- State tax credit for residential solar and wind energy systems, small wind, solar passive, solar space heat, and pool heating.
- State tax deduction for qualifying wood stove purchase; converting an existing wood fireplace to a qualifying wood stove.

INCENTIVES

- Arizona Public Services (APS)
- Duncan Valley Electric Cooperative
- Mohave Electric Cooperative
- Salt River Project
- Sulphur Springs Valley Electric Cooperative
- Trico Electric
- Tucson Electric Power (TEP)
- UniSource Electric (UES)

ARKANSAS

POLICY

- Net metering available on all renewable energy sources; credited to customer's next bill at retail rate; credits can be carried forward indefinitely.

- PACE financing approved by state legislation. Loan programs are established by municipality.

INCENTIVES

- Arkansas Oklahoma Gas (AOG)
- Entergy Arkansas
- First Electric Cooperative
- North Arkansas Electric Cooperative
- Southwestern Electric Power Co. (SWEPCO)

CALIFORNIA

POLICY

- California Solar Initiative implements a homebuyer solar program that requires sellers of production homes to offer a solar energy system option to all prospective homebuyers, and provide the cost of installation and estimated cost savings.
- County Wind Ordinance Standards authorizes counties to adopt provisions for wind energy systems.
- Fuel Mix Disclosure must be distributed to customers annually.
- Lancaster (City of) requires solar photovoltaics to be installed on new homes. Lancaster was the first U.S. city to adopt such a requirement, which became effective January 1, 2014.
- Net metering permitted on all renewable energy sources. Customers own RECs.
- PACE financing approved by state legislation. Loan programs are established by municipality.
- Property tax exclusion for solar energy systems for water heating, photovoltaic, and thermal electric. Pool and hot-tub heating systems are not eligible.

INCENTIVES

- Anaheim Public Utilities
- Burbank Water and Power
- Glendale Water and Power
- Imperial Irrigation District
- Lassen Municipal Utility District
- Lodi Electric

- Lompoc (City of)
- Los Angeles Dept. of Water and Power
- Marin County
- Modesto Irrigation District
- Pacific Gas and Electric
- Palo Alto (City of)
- Pasadena (City of)
- Plumas-Sierra REC
- Redding (City of)
- Riverside Public Utilities
- Roseville
- Sacramento Municipal Utility District (SMUD)
- Santa Clara Water and Sewage Utility
- San Diego County
- San Diego Gas and Electric
- San Francisco (City of)
- Silicon Valley Power (for residents of Santa Clara)
- SoCalGas
- Truckee Donnar Public Utility
- Ukiah Utilities

COLORADO

POLICY

- Boulder (City of) sales tax exemption for purchase of solar photovoltaic and solar water heating systems. Solar access to sunlight policy.
- Colorado Community Solar program enables residents to subscribe to off-site solar array or participate in a community solar garden.
- Colorado solar access law voids any covenants, restrictions or conditions that prohibit renewable energy generation devices or energy-efficient measures, including solar and wind generators that meet the state's interconnection standards. Certain cities have additional ordinances.
- Net metering allowed for all renewable energy systems. Customer owns RECs.
- PACE financing approved by state legislation. Loan programs are established by municipality.

- Property tax exemption for solar hot water, solar space heat, solar photovoltaics, wind, biomass, and geothermal heat pumps. Incentives administered by individual cities and counties.
- Sales tax exemption for purchase of any fixture or device for all solar, geothermal, wind, or biomass renewable energy systems.

INCENTIVES

- Aspen (City of)
- Atmos Energy
- Black Hills Energy
- Boulder County Elevations Energy
- Colorado Energy Office / Elevations Credit Union
- Colorado Natural Gas
- Colorado Springs Utilities
- Delta-Montrose Electric Association
- Denver (City of)
- Eagle County
- Efficiency Works
- Empire Electric
- Energy Smart Colorado / High Country Conservation Center
- Fort Collins Utilities
- Garfield County
- Gunnison County Electric
- Holy Cross Energy
- Lake County
- La Plata Electric Association
- Longmont Power & Communications
- Loveland Water and Power
- Morgan County Rural Electric Association
- Mountain View Electric Association
- Pitkin County
- Poudre Valley Rural Electric Association (PVREA)
- Roaring Fork Valley Energy Smart program
- San Miguel Power Association
- Sangre De Cristo Electric
- Southeast Colorado Power Association (SECPA)
- United Power
- Xcel Energy

CONNECTICUT

POLICY

- Libraries throughout Connecticut provide residents the opportunity to borrow a free *Kill-A-Watt* kit, provided by Eversource. Kits include instructions and a device to measure the energy use of an appliance.
- Net metering allowed for all renewable energy. Customers own RECs.
- PACE financing approved by state legislation. Loan programs are established by municipality.
- Permit fee exemption for all renewable energy systems may be authorized by local municipalities.
- Property tax exemption statewide for any type of renewable energy.
- Sales tax exemption for purchase of Energy Star water heaters, furnaces, boilers, windows, doors, insulation, programmable thermostats, and weatherization products.

INCENTIVES

- Capital for Change, Inc.
- Connecticut Green Bank
- Connecticut Light and Power / Energy Efficiency Fund
- Light & Power Co.
- Eversource
- United Illuminating Co.
- Energize Connecticut
- Groton Utilities
- Norwich Public Utilities
- Southern Connecticut Gas

DELAWARE

POLICY

- Net metering permitted by state policy for all renewable energy systems. Customer owns RECs.
- Solar rights law prohibits private covenants such as homeowners' associations from restricting use solar systems. Specifications apply.
- Wind access and permitting standards law prohibits unreasonable public and private restrictions on installation of wind energy systems on single-family residential properties meeting certain specifications.

INCENTIVES

- Delaware Dept. of Natural Resources and Environmental Control
- Electric Cooperative (DEC)
- Delaware Sustainable Energy Utility (SEU)
- Delmarva Power
- Energize Delaware Home Energy Loan Program
- Delaware Sustainable Utility / Delaware Dept. of Natural Resources and Environmental Control
- Sustainable Electric Utility (SEU)

DISTRICT OF COLUMBIA

POLICY

- Fuel mix disclosure must be provided to customers twice annually.
- Net metering allowed for all renewable energy systems. Compensation of excess energy based on size of generator.
- PACE financing approved by state legislation. Loan programs are established by municipality.
- Property tax exemption for purchase of solar water heat, space heat, thermal electric, solar photovoltaics, and combined heat and power.

INCENTIVES

- District of Columbia Sustainable Energy Utility (DCSEU)

FLORIDA

POLICY

- Florida laws include solar and wind access policies to protect homeowners from certain restrictions regarding wind or solar systems; includes certain prohibited rules of homeowners' associations.
- Net metering allowed for all renewable energy. Customer owns RECs.
- PACE financing approved by state legislation. Loan programs are established by municipality.
- Property tax exemption of 100% of installation cost of any type of solar, wind, or geothermal energy system.
- Sales tax exemption for purchase of solar energy systems.

INCENTIVES

- Beaches Energy Services
- Clay Electric
- Electric
- Duke Energy
- Florida Keys Electric Cooperative
- Florida Public Utilities
- Fort Pierce Utilities Authority
- Gainesville Regional Utilities
- Gulf Power
- JEA Solar Incentive
- Kissimmee Utility Authority
- Lakeland Electric
- Lauderhill (City of)
- New Smyrna Beach
- Ocala Utility Services
- Orlando Utilities
- Solar Energy Loan Fund
- Tallahassee Utilities
- Tampa Electric
- Winter Park (City of)

GEORGIA

POLICY

- Net Metering permitted by state policy for all renewable energy systems. Excess generation credited to customer's next bill.
- PACE Financing approved by state legislation. Loan programs are established by municipality.
- Sales tax exemption for purchase of biomass materials.
- Solar Easements law allows homeowners to negotiate for assurance of continued access to sunlight.

INCENTIVES

- Blue Ridge Mountain EMC and TVA
- Central Georgia EMC
- Coweta-Fayette Electric Membership Corp. (EMC)
- Diverse Power
- Electric Power Board

- Georgia Power Home
- Jackson Electric Membership Corp. (EMC)
- Marietta Power and Water
- Satilla EMC
- Swanee Energy
- Walton EMC

HAWAII

POLICY

- Hawaii provides residents with the *Energy Tax Credit,* a personal income tax credit based on 20% of the cost of equipment and installation of a wind system; and/or 35% of cost of solar thermal heating or photovoltaic system. Certain restrictions based on property type.
- Net metering is available on all solar photovoltaics, wind, biomass, and hydroelectric systems. Excess generation is credited to next bill.
- PACE financing approved by state legislation. Loan programs are established by municipality.
- Solar access law prohibits covenants or restrictions that restrict the installation of a solar energy system on a residential dwelling or townhouse.
- Homeowners' associations must adopt rules regarding placement of solar energy systems.

INCENTIVES

- Hawaii Community Reinvestment Corporation
- Hawaii Energy
- Honolulu (City and County) *Solar Loan*
- Kauai Island Utility Cooperative (KIUC)
- KIUC Solar Water Rebate Program

IDAHO

POLICY

- Net metering is available through Rocky Mountain Power and Avista Utilities.
- Solar easement law places restrictions to homeowners' association rules regarding solar panels or collectors on property rooftops that are owned and maintained by the homeowner.
- State income tax deduction for alternative energy for solar, wind, geothermal, and certain biomass devices for heating or electrical generation.
- State income tax deduction for efficiency upgrades on homes built or under construction before 2002 and certain other criteria.

LOANS

- Idaho Governor's Office of Energy Resources offers low-interest loans for home improvements to conserve energy.
- Idaho Falls Power residential energy-efficient loan program for upgrades of water heaters, heat pumps, insulation, and air conditioners.

INCENTIVES

- Avista Utilities (Electric)
- Idaho Falls Power
- Idaho Power
- Kootenai Electric Cooperative
- Intermountain Gas Company
- Northern Lights
- Questar Gas
- Rocky Mountain
- Kootenai Electrical Cooperative

ILLINOIS

POLICY

- Net metering; renewable energy credits (RECs) and bill crediting.
- PACE financing approved by state legislation. Loan programs are established by municipality.
- Property tax special assessment for solar energy systems.

- Solar and Wind Rights access policy prohibits homeowners' associations and common-interest community associations from preventing homeowners from using or installing solar energy systems but may set location and other specifications. Associations may restrict all wind devices.

INCENTIVES

- Ameren
- City of Chicago, *Green Building Permit*
- City Water Light and Power
- Commonwealth Edison
- Corn Belt Energy Cooperative
- Jo-Carroll Energy Cooperative
- MidAmerican Energy
- Nicor Gas
- North Shore Gas
- Peoples Gas
- Wabash Valley Power Association

INDIANA

POLICY

- Net metering permitted for solar thermal electric, solar photovoltaics, wind, biomass, hydroelectric, and other renewable energy sources.
- Property tax exemption for renewable heating or cooling systems including solar, wind, or hydropower.
- Solar easements and rights law prevents planning and zoning authorities from prohibiting or unreasonably restricting use of solar energy.
- State income tax deduction for building insulation and solar-powered roof vents or fans installed on homeowner's principal residence.

INCENTIVES

- Bartholomew County REMC
- Carroll County REMC
- Carroll White REMC
- Citizens Gas
- Clark County REMC
- Dubois REC
- Duke Energy
- Harrison County REMC

- Jackson County REMC
- Jay County REMC
- Johnson County REMC
- Marshall County REMC
- NineStar Connect
- NIPSCO Gas & Electric
- Noble REMC
- Northeastern REMC
- Orange County REMC
- Parke County REMC
- RushShelby Energy
- South Central Indiana
- Southeastern Indiana REMC
- Southern Indiana Power
- Tipmont REMC
- Vectren Energy
- Wabash County REMC
- Western Indiana Utilities District

IOWA

POLICY

- Net metering programs are available through MidAmerican Energy and Alliant Energy.
- Personal income tax credits for solar energy or geothermal heat pump; various rules apply.
- Property tax exemption for renewable energy systems, various rules apply.
- Sales tax exemption for purchase of solar, wind and hydroelectric equipment.
- Solar easement provision allows access to sunlight and permits home-owners to obtain voluntary easements from a property owner or apply to a regulatory board; in absence of a board, matter can be referred to local district court.

INCENTIVES

- Alliant Energy Interstate Power and Light
- Ames Electric
- Black Hills Energy (Gas)

- Cedar Fall Utilities
- Farmers Electric Cooperative (Kalona)
- Indianola Municipal Utilities
- Liberty Utilities Iowa
- Linn County Rural Electric Cooperative
- MidAmerican Energy
- Muscatine Power and Water
- Waverly Light and Power

KANSAS

POLICY

- Net metering available for solar thermal electric, solar photovoltaics, wind, hydroelectric, and other renewable systems.
- Property tax exemption for installation of geothermal, solar electric, solar photovoltaic, wind, and other renewable energy systems.
- Solar easement statute allows parties to voluntarily enter into solar easement contracts for the purpose of ensuring adequate exposure of a solar energy system.

INCENTIVES

- Midwest Energy *How$mart Energy Efficiency Finance Program*

KENTUCKY

POLICY

- Net metering available for solar photovoltaic, wind, hydroelectric, and other renewable energy systems.
- PACE financing approved by state legislation. Loan programs are established by municipality.
- Solar easements may be obtained for the purpose of ensuring access to direct sunlight; must be in writing and will become an interest in real property that may be acquired and transferred.
- State income tax credit on installations of water heaters, lighting, furnaces, boilers, heat pumps, air conditioners, insulation, windows, and doors meeting certain energy efficiency ratings. Amounts capped by equipment type.

INCENTIVES

- Blue Grass Energy
- Clark Energy
- Columbia Gas of Kentucky
- Community Assistance Resources for Energy Savings (CARES)
- Cumberland Valley Electric Cooperative
- Duke Energy
- Farmers RECC
- Grayson Rural Electric Cooperative
- Inter-County Energy Cooperative
- Jackson Energy
- Mountain Assn. for Community Economic Development
- Nolin RECC
- Owen Electric
- Salt River Electric
- Southern Kentucky RECC
- Taylor County RECC

LOUISIANA

POLICY

- Net metering available for solar photovoltaic, wind, hydroelectric, and other renewable energy systems; similar rule adopted by New Orleans City Council.
- Solar energy system property tax exemption by LA Dept. of Revenue excludes solar energy systems in homes and swimming pools.
- Solar rights legislation prohibits certain entities from unreasonably restricting a property owner from installing a solar collector. Exceptions apply to historic districts, preservation areas, and designated landmarks.

INCENTIVES

- Cleco
- Dixie Electric Membership Corp. (DEMCO)
- Entergy (Louisiana and Gulf States)
- Entergy New Orleans
- Louisiana Dept of Natural Resources *Home Energy Loan Program*
- Southwestern Electric Power Co. (SWEPCO)

MAINE

POLICY

- Efficiency Maine *Residential Lighting Program* is a statewide program in collaboration with retailers, manufacturers, and distributors.
- Fuel Mix and Emissions Disclosure must be sent to customers four times per year.
- Libraries throughout Maine provide residents the opportunity to borrow a free *Kill-A-Watt Kit*, provided by Efficiency Maine. Kits include instructions and a device to measure the energy use of an appliance.
- *Model Wind Energy Ordinance* provides a number of ordinances that may be used by local governments to help facilitate wind development.
- Net metering law includes a buy-all, sell-all compensation program for new distributed generation customers, where a customer's total system production and total household consumption are credited and billed at separate rates. Law applies to solar, wind, hydro, and other renewable energy.
- PACE financing available and administered locally or by Efficiency Maine Trust.
- Solar easements law allows the creation of easements to ensure access to direct sunlight. Easements must be recorded and indexed the same way as conveyances of real property.
- Solar rights for residential properties apply to homeowners' associations whereby homeowners may not be prohibited from installing or using a solar energy device. The policy protects a renter's rights to use a clothesline or drying rack.

INCENTIVES

- Efficiency Maine *Appliance Rebate Program*
- Efficiency Maine *Home Energy Savings Program (HESP)*

MARYLAND

POLICY

- Energy storage tax credit enables taxpayers who install energy storage systems to receive a tax credit of 30% of the installed cost up to $5,000. Application and certificates are processed through Maryland Energy Administration.
- Fuel mix and emissions disclosure must be provided to customers twice yearly.
- Net metering is permitted on all renewable energy systems.
- PACE financing approved by state legislation. Loan programs are established by municipality.
- Property taxes are exempt from state (not local) homes with solar and wind energy systems.
- Renewable energy certificates (RECs) and solar renewable energy certificates (SRECs) and RECs are owned by the customer.
- Sales tax exemption for wood-heating fuel or refuse-derived fuels such as biomass.
- Sales tax holiday for purchase of certain energy-efficient appliances occurs for 3 days annually beginning on the Saturday immediately preceding the third Monday in February.
- Solar easements and rights laws prohibit unreasonable limitations on the installation of solar collection panels on the roof or exterior walls of homes; historic properties excluded.
- State law allows counties and municipalities to provide a property tax credit for high performance and green building, including solar, wind, geothermal, and hydroelectric systems. Jurisdictions can specify which renewable energy source.
- Tax credits for solar energy and geothermal systems are provided by the following counties: Montgomery County, Howard County, Baltimore County, and Anne Arundel County.

INCENTIVES

- Baltimore Gas and Electric
- Delmarva Power
- FirstEnergy (Potomac Edison)

- Maryland Dept. of Housing and Community Development *BeSMART Home Energy Loan Program; Net Zero Construction Loan Program;* and *EmPOWER Program.*
- Maryland Energy Administration's *Clean Energy Grant Program*; and *Low-to-Moderate Income Energy Efficiency Grant.*
- Potomac Electric Power Company (PEPCO)
- Southern Maryland Electric Cooperative (SEMCO)

MASSACHUSETTS

POLICY

- Fuel mix and emissions disclosure must be sent to customers on a quarterly basis and upon request.
- Income tax credit allows homeowners to receive a 15% credit up to $1,000 for the installation of a renewable energy system on the individual's primary residence.
- Net metering is mandatory for investor-owned utility companies and may be offered by municipal utilities. Rules based on system capacity and customers owns renewable energy certificates (RECs). Aggregate and neighborhood net metering permitted.
- PACE financing approved by state legislation. Loan programs are established by municipality.
- Property tax exemption for homes with installed solar, hydro, or wind energy systems. Subject to terms and conditions.
- Sales tax exemption on purchase of any solar, wind, geothermal, or other renewable heat pump system.
- Solar easement rights law permits voluntary agreements to prohibit unreasonable restrictions to solar access, but the law does not make solar access an automatic right. Statute allows communities to authorize zoning boards to issue permits creating solar rights.

INCENTIVES

- Berkshire Gas
- Cape Light Compact (CLC)
- Chicopee Electric Light Dept.
- Concord Municipal Light Plant
- Eversource

- Holyoke Gas and Electric
- Liberty Utilities
- Mansfield Municipal Electric Dept.
- Marblehead Municipal Light Dept.
- Massachusetts Clean Energy Center
- Mass Save Program
- Massachusetts Municipal Wholesale Electric Company, *MuniHELP*S
- National Grid
- Reading Municipal Light Dept. (RMLD
- Shrewsbury Electric
- Taunton Municipal Lighting Plant
- Unitil
- Wakefield Municipal Gas and Light Dept.
- Wellesley Municipal Light Plant

MICHIGAN

POLICY

- Fuel mix emissions disclosure must be provided to customers twice annually.
- Net metering permitted statewide for all renewable energy systems. Customer owns renewable energy certificates (RECs).

INCENTIVES

- Alger-Delta Electric
- Bay City Electric Light and Power
- Charlevoix (City of)
- Chelsea Electric Department
- Cloverland Electric
- Coldwater Board of Public Utilities
- Consumers Energy Company (Electric)
- Consumers Energy Company (Gas)
- Croswell Light and Power Department
- Daggett Electric
- Detroit Edison Company (DTE Energy)
- Eaton (City of)
- Efficiency Gas United
- Escanaba (City of)
- Grand Haven Board of Light and Power
- Great Lakes Energy
- Great Lakes Energy Cooperative

- Hart Hydro-Electric
- HomeWorks Tri-County Electric Cooperative
- Lansing Board of Water and Light
- Lowell Light and Power
- Marquette Board of Light and Power
- Michigan Electric Cooperative Association (MECA)
- Michigan Saves
- Midwest Energy Cooperative
- Newberry Water and Light Board
- Niles Utility Department
- Ontonagon County Rural Electrification Association
- Paw Paw (Village of)
- Portland Light and Power Board
- Presque Isle Electric and Gas Cooperative
- South Haven (City of)
- St. Louis (City of)
- Stephenson (City of)
- Sturgis (City of)
- Wyandotte Municipal Services
- Zeeland Board of Public Works

MINNESOTA

POLICY

- Fuel mix and emissions disclosure must be provided twice annually; utilities may distribute information electronically.
- Net metering permitted for all renewable energy sources and apply to all utility companies. Customers own RECs.
- PACE financing approved by state legislation. Loan programs are established by municipality.
- Sales tax exemption on solar and wind energy equipment.
- Solar and wind access policy is specially defined for the City of Minneapolis.
- Solar and wind easements may be created for solar and wind energy systems, and local zoning board may create variances and restrictions.
- Solar and wind property tax exemption on equipment; other restrictions apply to land on which system is located.

INCENTIVES

- Alexandria Light and Power
- Anoka Municipal Utility
- Austin Gas and Electric
- Bloomington Prairie Public Utilities
- Brainerd Public Utilities
- Center Point Energy
- Connexus Energy
- Crow Wing Electric
- Dakota Electric Association
- East Central Energy
- Elk River Municipal Utilities
- Fairmount Public Utilities
- Grand Marais
- Great River Energy
- Hutchinson Utilities Commission
- Lake Cities
- Lake Country Power
- Litchfield Public Utilities
- Marshall Municipal
- Minnesota Center for Energy and Environment
- Minnesota Housing Finance Agency *Fix-Up Fund*
- Minnesota Power
- Minnesota Valley Electric
- Moorehead Public Service Utility
- Mora Municipal Utilities
- New Prague Utilities Commission
- New Ulm Public Utilities
- North Branch Municipal Water and Light
- Owatanna Public Utilities
- Preston Public Utilities
- Princeton PUC
- Redwood Falls Public Utilities
- Renewable Energy Standard
- Rochester Public Utilities
- Saint Peter Municipal Utilities
- Shakopee Public Utilities
- Spring Valley Public Utilities
- Stearns Electric Association
- Waseca Utilities
- Wells Public Utilities

- Wilmar Municipal Utilities
- Wilmar Public Utilities
- Wright-Hennepin Cooperative Electric
- Xcel Energy

MISSISSIPPI

POLICY

- Net metering available for all renewable energy systems. Various terms for excess generation and RECs ownership and transfer.

INCENTIVES

- Atmos Energy
- Coast Electric Power Association
- Entergy Mississippi
- Mississippi Power
- Pearl River Valley Electric Power Association
- Singing River Electric Power Association
- Southern Pine Electric Power Association

MISSOURI

POLICY

- Kansas City access policy requires owners to negotiate with other property owners for desired easements to protect sunlight access; Kansas City municipal code permits geothermal systems in all zoning districts.

- Net metering is available on all renewable energy systems. Excess energy is credited to customer's next bill at avoided-cost rate.

- PACE financing approved by state legislation. Loan programs are established by municipality. *Set the PACE St. Louis* enables certain residential property owners with no existing mortgage to obtain PACE financing up to 35% of property value. Alternative options available. Administered by Energy Equity Funding, LLC on behalf of the St. Louis Clean Energy Development Board.

- Property tax exemption on 100% of costs of energy systems consisting of solar water heat, solar space heat, solar thermal electric, solar thermal process heat, and solar photovoltaics. State, local, and county property taxes exempt.

- Sales tax holiday for energy-efficient appliances. Annual 7-day sales tax exemption from April 19 to April 25 on certain Energy Star certified new appliances. Personal or business use; up to $1,500 per appliance.
- Solar access policy gives property owners a right to utilize solar energy, but eminent domain may not be used to obtain such a property right. Easements for a solar energy system must be created in writing and are subject conveyance and instrument recording.
- State income tax deduction for home energy audits and associated energy improvements. $1,000 limit per individual; $2,000 joint returns.

INCENTIVES

- Ameren Missouri Electric
- Citizens Electric Corporation
- City Utilities of Springfield
- Co-Mo Electric Cooperative
- Columbia Water and Light
- Cuivre River Electric
- Empire District
- Independence Power and Light
- Intercounty Electric Cooperative
- Kansas City Power and Light
- Kirkwood Electric
- Liberty Utilities
- Missouri Rural Electric Cooperative
- Ozark Border Electric Cooperative
- Platt-Clay Electric Cooperative
- Southwest Electric
- Spire Energy
- Wabash Valley Power Association
- White River Valley Electric Cooperative

MONTANA

POLICY

- Net metering permitted for solar photovoltaics, all wind, and hydroelectric. Excess generation credited to customer's next bill at retail rate.
- Personal tax credit of 100% of investment up to $1,500 for geothermal heat pumps.

- Personal tax credit of 25% of capital investment up to $500 for individual or $1,000 for joint filers for installation of energy-conservation equipment including doors, windows, insulation, water heaters, lighting, furnaces, boilers, heat recovery, air conditioners, air sealing, weather-stripping, LED lighting, and programmable thermostats.
- Property tax exemption available for recognized non-fossil forms of energy generation and low emission wood or biomass combustion devices. Up to $20,000 or 100% of investment value for 10 years for single-family homes.
- Solar and wind easement provisions allow property owners to create solar and wind easements for the purpose of protecting and maintaining proper access to sunlight and wind. Solar easements should be negotiated with neighboring property owners.

INCENTIVES

- Alternative Energy Revolving Loan Program
- Flathead Electric Cooperative
- Montana-Dakota Utilities
- Northwestern Energy
- Yellowstone Valley Electric Cooperative

NEBRASKA

POLICY

- Net metering available. Customers own RECs and excess generation credited to next bill.
- PACE financing approved by state legislation. Loan programs are established by municipality.
- Solar and wind access provisions allow property owners to create binding easements for the purpose of protecting proper access to sunlight and wind.

INCENTIVES

- Lincoln Electrical System
- MidAmerican Energy (Gas)
- Nebraska Dollar and Energy Savings
- Nebraska Public Power District
- Southern Power District

NEVADA

POLICY

- Fuel mix and emissions disclosure must be provided twice annually.
- Net metering available. Customers own RECs unless utility subsidizes system; various policies for excess generation credits.
- PACE financing approved by state legislation. Residential programs not addressed.
- Solar and wind access provisions disallow covenants, deeds, contracts, ordinances or other legal instruments which unreasonably restrict property owners from using a solar or wind energy system.

INCENTIVES

- NV Energy (Northern Nevada)
- NV Energy Solar Thermal Heating Program
- NV Energy, Energy Storage Incentive Program
- Southwest Gas Corporation

NEW HAMPSHIRE

POLICY

- Fuel mix and emissions disclosure must be provided annually.
- Net metering available. Customers own RECs unless utility subsidizes system; various policies for excess generation credits.
- New Hampshire allows cities and towns to offer an exemption from local property taxes for the assessed value of a solar energy system, electrical energy storage system, wind energy system, or wood-fired central heating system on the property.
- New Hampshire's *Solar Skyspace Easement* provision allows property owners to create solar easements to preserve a right to unobstructed access to solar energy. Easements remain in effect for at least 10 years.
- New Hampshire Municipal Small Wind Regulations Ordinance prevents municipalities from adopting ordinances or regulations that place unreasonable limits on or hinder the performance of wind energy systems up to 100 kilowatts (kW) in capacity. Such wind turbines must be used primarily to produce energy for on-site consumption.

- PACE financing approved by state legislation. Residential programs not addressed.

INCENTIVES

- New Hampshire Public Utilities Commission provides incentives under the following programs: *Renewable Energy Rebate Program; Solar Water-heating Rebate Program; Bulk-fed Wood Pellet Central Boilers and Furnaces Rebate Program.*

- Eversource
- Liberty Utilities (Electric)
- New Hampshire Electric Co-op
- Unitil (Electric)
- Unitil (Gas)

NEW JERSEY

POLICY

- Fuel mix and emissions disclosure must be provided to customers on bills, contracts and marketing materials. No specific frequency.

- Net metering available. Customers own RECs; excess generation credited to customer's next bill at retail rate. NJ permits solar renewable energy certificates (SRCs) and transition renewable energy certificates (TRECs).

- PACE financing approved by state legislation. Loan programs are established by municipality.

- Property tax exemptions of 100% of value of any type installed renewable energy system; property owners obtain certificate from their local assessor.

- Sales tax exemption for 100% of cost of solar energy equipment and devices for passive, thermal, process or photovoltaic systems; solar pool heating.

- Solar access provisions allow for the creation of solar easements to ensure that proper sunlight is available to those who operate solar-energy systems. Legislation prevents homeowners' associations from prohibiting solar collectors on certain property types.

- Wind access provisions prevent municipalities from adopting regulations that place unreasonable limits or hinder the performance of small wind energy systems; devices must be used primary to produce on-site energy consumption.

INCENTIVES

New Jersey Office of Clean Energy offers the following programs:

- *Comfort Partners Program; COOL Advantage Program*
- *Home Performance with Energy Star*
- *New Construction Program*
- *WARM Advantage Program*
- New Jersey Board of Public Utilities, *Energy Star program*
- New Jersey Natural Gas *SAVEGREEN Project*
- PSE&G offers NJ Clean Energy *Cool Advantage* & *Warm Advantage*
- South Jersey Gas

NEW MEXICO

POLICY

- Farmington (City of) offers net metering credits on solar, hydro, wind, and other distributed energy technologies.
- Net metering available. Customers own RECs; excess generation credited to customer's next bill at avoided cost rate.
- PACE financing approved by state legislation. Loan programs are established by municipality.
- Personal tax credit available for owners of sustainable buildings; tax credit computed according to LEED efficiency ratings and square footage use sectors. Renewable energy tax credits were previously available and administered by Clean Energy Incentives, New Mexico Energy, Minerals and Natural Resources.
- Property tax exemptions are available for homes with installed solar water heat, space heat, and photovoltaics. Annual increases to property assessment values are incrementally structured.
- Sales tax exemption for solar energy equipment and installation for passive, thermal, process or photovoltaic systems.
- Solar Rights Act and Solar Recordation Act allow property owners to create solar easements for the purpose of protecting and maintaining proper access to sunlight, and established the right to use solar energy as a property right. Law prevents neighboring property owners from constructing new buildings or planting new trees which would block sunlight to solar collectors.

INCENTIVES

- Central New Mexico Electric Cooperative
- El Paso Electric Company
- New Mexico Energy Saver program
- New Mexico Gas Company
- Public Service Company of New Mexico (PNM)
- Xcel Energy, appliance rebates

NEW YORK

POLICY

- Fuel mix and emissions disclosure must be provided every 6 months.
- Net metering is permitted; excess generation credit to customer's next bill at retail rates; other restrictions based on energy type and features. RECs have certain restrictions. Solar net metering is available through Consolidated Edison, National Grid, PSE&G.
- PACE financing approved by state legislation. Loan programs are established by municipality.
- Personal income tax credit for purchase and installation of solar energy systems. Credits available on both purchased systems and leases through a power purchase agreement.
- Property tax abatement available for solar photovoltaic systems installed on residential homes located in New York City, and cities with a population of 1 million or more people.
- Property tax exemption available (by local adoption) for Green Buildings that meet energy standards by LEED or equivalent certification.
- Property tax exemption for energy efficiency improvements, including electric energy storage and systems. Applicable to a variety of measures on 1-4 family homes.
- Property tax exemption for installation of any type of renewable energy system; 100% exemption for 15 years. Local municipalities may approve or opt out.
- Solar easements may be created voluntarily to ensure uninterrupted solar access for solar energy devices; agreements must contain location and orientation to property and other provisions. Cities, towns, and villages in New York are allowed to make regulations to accommodate access to sunlight.

INCENTIVES

- New York State Energy Research and Development Authority administers the *Home Performance with Energy Star* program through the following participating utilities: Central Hudson, Con Edison, PSEG-Long Island, National Grid (upstate customers), NY State Electric and Gas (Orange and Rockland) and Rochester Gas and Electric.
- New York State Energy Research Authority offers several programs: the *Renewable Heat NY* program wood-burning program, funded by Regional Greenhouse Gas Initiative; and *NY Sun Incentive Program* for the solar thermal and PV systems; *Small Wind* systems incentives paid to installers, who pass on savings to customers.
- New York State Homes and Community Renewal, loans through the State of New York Mortgage Agency.
- *New York Sun Initiative,* loans through Energy Finance Solutions.
- Town of Babylon offers the *Long Island Green Homes* program.
- Rebates or other financial incentives are available from:
    - Central Hudson Gas and Electric
    - Consolidated Edison
    - National Fuel (gas)
    - National Grid (gas)
    - National Grid (upstate)
    - New York State Electric and Gas Corp.
    - Orange and Rockland Utilities
    - PSE&G Long Island
    - Rochester Gas and Electric

NORTH CAROLINA

POLICY

- Net metering available; utility owns RECs unless customer chooses other option; excess generation credited on next bill at retail rate.
- PACE financing approved by state legislation. Loan programs are established by municipality.
- Property tax exemption for active solar heating and cooling systems.
- Solar rights ordinance was adopted by the Town of Chapel Hill prohibiting covenants by neighborhood or homeowners' associations that restrict or prohibit the use, installation, or maintenance of solar-collection devices.

- Solar rights ordinances may be adopted by cities and counties to prohibit certain types of installation features and locations.
- Wind ordinances that regulate the use of wind-energy systems have been adopted by the following jurisdictions in North Carolina:
    - Ashe County
    - Carteret County
    - Currituck County
    - Hyde County
    - Kill Devil Hills (Town of)
    - Madison County
    - Pitt County
    - Tyrell County
    - Watauga County

INCENTIVES

- Carteret-Craven Electric Cooperative
- Concord (City of)
- Duke Energy (Electric)
- Duke Energy Progress, Energy Star rebates
- Duke Energy (Solar rebates)
- Energy United (Electric)
- Energy United (Gas)
- Four County EMC
- Heywood EMC
- High Point (City of) Electric
- Jones-Oslow EMC
- Lumbee River EMC
- New Bern (City of) Electric Department
- Piedmont EMC
- Piedmont Natural Gas
- PSNC Energy (Gas)
- South River EMC
- Statesville (City of) Electric Utility Dept.
- Tideland EMC
- Union Power Cooperative

NORTH DAKOTA

POLICY

- Net metering available; customers own RECs; excess generation reconciled monthly at avoided cost rate.
- Property tax exemptions are available to property owners with installed qualified solar, wind, or geothermal energy systems and devices. Exemptions apply to local assessments for the 5-year period following installation.
- Solar easement law allows property owners to obtain a written agreement from another property owner for the purpose of ensuring adequate exposure to sunlight.
- Wind easement statute authorizes residential property owners to create wind easements to ensure access to wind, as well as address other provisions to protect the homeowner.

INCENTIVES

- Bright Energy Solutions offers rebates for purchase of energy-efficient appliances to customers of utility companies that are members of Missouri River Energy Services. North Dakota members include: Cavalier Municipal Utilities, Hillsboro Municipal Utilities, Lakota Municipal Light Plant, Northwood Municipal Utilities, and Valley City Public Works.
- Excel Energy offers rebates for energy-efficient water heaters, boilers, and furnaces.
- Otter Tail Power Company offers rebates for installation of energy efficient water heating, furnaces, heat pumps, and thermal storage technologies.

OHIO

POLICY

- Cincinnati (City of) property tax abatement for homes constructed or renovated to meet LEED certification standards.
- Cleveland (City of) property tax abatement for homes built in accordance with the Cleveland Green Building Standard.
- Net metering available; excess generation credited to customer's next bill at unbundled generation rate.

- PACE financing approved by state legislation. Loan programs are established by municipality.
- Solar easement law allows property owners to obtain a written agreement from another property owner for the purpose of ensuring adequate exposure to sunlight.
- Solar renewable energy certificates (SRECs) are eligible.
- Wind farms above 5 MW in capacity must receive a permit from Ohio Power Siting Board; setback requirements. Wind farms below 5 MW are subject to local ordinances and not state jurisdiction.

INCENTIVES

- American Municipal Power
- Butler Rural Electric Cooperative
- Columbia Gas of Ohio
- Consolidated Electric Cooperative
- Dayton Power and Light
- Dominion East Ohio (Gas)
- Duke Energy (Gas & Electric), *Smart$ave* program
- Energy Conservation for Ohioans (ECO-link)
- Firelands Electric Cooperative
- Hamilton County *Home Improvement Program*
- The Energy Cooperative
- Vectren Energy Delivery of Ohio (Gas)

OKLAHOMA

POLICY

- Net metering available; excess generation compensated at avoided cost rate.
- PACE financing approved by state legislation. Loan programs are established by county. Property owners must obtain an energy audit; efficiency equipment must be Energy Star rated.

INCENTIVES

- AEP Public Service Company of Oklahoma
- CenterPoint (Gas)
- East Central Electrical Cooperative
- Oklahoma City *Green Home Loan Program*
- Oklahoma Gas and Electric (OG&E)
- Oklahoma Electric Cooperative

- Oklahoma Municipal Power Authority
- Oklahoma Natural Gas
- Red River Valley Rural Electric Cooperative
- Verdigris Valley Electrical Cooperative

OREGON

POLICY

- Ashland (City of) has specific setback provisions for solar energy.
- Eugene (City of) has specific lot standards for new home construction for the purpose of promoting the use of solar energy.
- Net metering available; customers own RECs unless subsidized by Energy Trust; excess generation credited on customer's next bill at retail rate, depending upon enrollment terms.
- PACE financing approved by state legislation. Loan programs are established by city or county.
- Portland (City of) offers a streamlined permitting process for residential solar energy system installations.
- Property tax exemption on homes with qualifying net-metered renewable energy system such as solar, geothermal, wind, water, fuel cell, etc. that are used to offset on-site electricity use.
- Solar and Wind access laws allow property owners to create solar and wind easements for the purpose of protecting and maintaining proper access to sunlight and wind. Easements are negotiated with neighboring property owners. Legislation voids any provisions of a planned community which prohibit installation and use of solar panels.

INCENTIVES

- Ashland Electric Utilities Department
- Central Lincoln People's Utility District
- Columbia River Power
- Consumer's Power, Inc.
- Douglas Electric Cooperative
- Emerald People's Utility District
- Energy Trust of Oregon (numerous programs)
- Eugene Water and Electric Board
- Forest Grove Light and Power
- Idaho Power
- Lane Electric Cooperative

- McMinnville Water and Light
- Midstate Electric Cooperative
- Oregon Trail Electric Cooperative
- Portland General Electric
- Salem Electric
- Springfield Utility Board
- State Home Oil
- Tillamook County PUD

PENNSYLVANIA

POLICY

- Net metering available; excess generation credited to customer's next bill at full retail rate; customer owns RECs; SRECs available.
- Fuel mix disclosure must be provided upon reasonable request by customer.

INCENTIVES

- Adams Electric Cooperative
- Duquesne Light Company
- FirstEnergy (Metedison, Penelec, Penn Power, West Penn Power)
- PECO Energy (Electric)
- PECO Energy (Gas)
- Philadelphia (City Of) Solar Rebate Program
- Philadelphia Gas Works
- PPL Electric Utilities

RHODE ISLAND

POLICY

- Fuel mix disclosure must be provided quarterly.
- Net metering available; excess generation rolled over to customer's next bill or purchased by utility.
- PACE financing approved by state legislation. Loan programs are established by local government.
- Property tax exemptions are applied to 100% of the cost of any installed renewable energy system including solar, wind, geothermal, small hydro, eligible biomass, and fuel cells.

- Sales tax exemptions are applied to the purchase of eligible products, including solar electric systems and connection devices, solar thermal systems, geothermal heat pumps, wind turbines and towers.
- Solar easements may be established by property owners and include required descriptions and provisions.

INCENTIVES

- National Grid offers free home energy assessments and rebates.

SOUTH CAROLINA

POLICY

- Net metering available; excess generation credited to customer's next bill on a monthly basis. Annual payout to customer at avoided cost and other terms.
- Personal tax credits of 25% of eligible costs are applied to the purchase and installation of a solar energy or small hydropower system for heating water, space heating, air cooling, and other home energy measures. Maximum per-year credits and other terms apply.
- Personal tax credits up to $750 are available to purchasers of a manufactured home that meets or exceeds the energy-efficiency requirements of an Energy Star program, or equivalent rating. Homes must be located in South Carolina and be purchased from a retail dealership licensed by the S.C. Manufactured Housing Board.

INCENTIVES

- Aiken Electric Cooperative
- Berkeley Electric Cooperative
- Blue Ridge Electric Cooperative
- Duke Energy (electric)
- Duke Energy *Customer Scale Solar Program*
- Duke Energy Progress *New Construction Program*
- Palmetto Electric *Buried Treasure Program*
- Pee Dee Electric
- Piedmont Natural Gas
- Rock Hill Utilities
- Santee Electric Cooperative
- SCE&G (electric) *EnergyWise Program*
- York Electric

SOUTH DAKOTA

POLICY

- South Dakota property owners may grant a solar or wind easement. Must be in writing and include certain descriptions; maximum term of 50 years.

INCENTIVES

- Black Hills Energy
- Otter Tail Power Company
- Montana-Dakota Utilities (Gas)
- Southeastern Electric Coop
- Big Stone City (City of)
- Burke (City of)
- Flandreau (City of)
- Fort Pierre (City of)
- Pierre (City of)
- Watertown Municipal Utilities
- Winner Municipal Utility

TENNESSEE

POLICY

- Solar easements may be created by property owners to ensure access to direct sunlight for solar energy systems. Tennessee law encourages counties and municipalities to promulgate zoning regulations that encourage and protect solar energy use.

INCENTIVES

- Bristol Tennessee Electric Service
- Electric Power Board of Chattanooga
- Murfreesboro Electric Department
- Middle Tennessee Electric

TEXAS

POLICY

- Austin (City of) provides height limitation exemption for solar installations which may exceed district height limit by 15%.
- Fuel mix disclosure must be provided upon request and in the form of a standardized Electricity Facts Label. Labels must be updated annually.
- Net metering available; offered through El Paso Electric; San Antonio City Public Service Energy; city of Brenham.
- PACE financing approved by state legislation. Loan programs are established by city or county. Residential not addressed.
- Property tax exemption based on 100% of appraisal value increase arising from installation or construction of a solar or wind-powered energy device for on-site use and storage.
- Sales tax exemption during Memorial Day weekend 3-day tax holiday for the purchase of certain Energy Star appliances.
- San Antonio (City of) has specific zoning standards for solar and wind energy systems.
- Solar easements law restricts homeowners' associations from restricting property owners from installing a solar energy device; certain exceptions are permitted.

INCENTIVES

- AEP SWEPCO
- AEP Texas Central Company
- AEP Texas North Company
- Austin Energy (numerous programs)
- Bandera Electric Cooperative
- Bryan Texas Utilities
- CenterPoint Energy
- College Station Utilities
- CoServ
- CPS Energy
- CPS Energy (Electric)
- Denton Municipal Electric
- El Paso Electric
- Entergy Texas
- Farmers Electric Cooperative
- Garland Power and Light

- Green Mountain Energy
- Guadalupe Valley Electric Cooperative
- New Braunfels Utilities
- Oncor Electric Delivery
- Pedernales Electric Cooperative
- San Marcos (City of)
- Sunset Valley (City of)
- Texas Gas Service
- Texas-New Mexico Power Company
- Tri-County Electric Cooperative
- United Cooperative Services
- Xcel Energy

UTAH

POLICY

- PACE financing approved by state legislation. Loan programs are established by city or county. Residential not addressed.
- Solar easements law permits parties to voluntarily enter into written solar easement contracts; must be in writing and duly recorded. Community associations rights are limited to ownership interest on the owner's property roof.
- Solar net metering; net billing; customer owns RECs; available through Rocky Mountain Power; City of St. George; Murray City Power.

INCENTIVES

- Rocky Mountain Power
- Dominion Energy

VERMONT

POLICY

- Net metering permitted; excess generation credited to customer's next bill at blended residential rate; utility owns RECs unless customer elects to retain ownership and agree to credit adjustment.
- PACE financing approved by state legislation. Loan programs are established by municipality. Loan limits apply.
- Property tax exemption may be offered by municipalities for certain renewable energy systems; state taxes still apply.

- Property tax exemptions available for solar PV systems up to 50 kilowatts and apply to statewide education property tax.
- Sales tax exemption for 100% of purchase cost of renewable energy system; applies to grid-tied and off-grid.
- Solar access law forbids ordinances, bylaws, deed restrictions, covenants, declarations, or similar binding agreements from prohibiting the use of solar collectors, clotheslines, or other energy devices based on renewable resources. Homeowners may be subject to certain restrictions regarding the location of solar collectors. Other rules apply.
- Solar photovoltaic permitting process is expedited; procedures vary according to system features and interconnection

INCENTIVES

- Burlington Electric Dept.
- Efficiency Vermont (numerous programs)
- Vermont Gas

VIRGINIA

POLICY

- Fuel mix disclosures must be provided once annually.
- Net metering available; customer owns RECs; excess generation credited to customer's next bill at retail rate. City of Danville has specific requirements.
- PACE financing approved by state legislation. Loan programs are established by local governments.
- Personal tax deduction based on a percentage of sales price is available on certain energy efficient equipment such as household appliances, heating systems and other devices.
- Property tax exemption may be created by any county, city, or town to exempt or partially exempt solar energy and recycling equipment from property taxes. Local jurisdictions may assess property tax of an energy-efficient building at a reduced rate. Properties must meet efficiency standards such as Energy Star, LEED, etc. or exceed statewide building codes by 30%. Local jurisdictions may impose revised property tax on renewable energy generating machinery and tools.

- Sales tax holiday exempts sales tax for Energy Star and WaterSense products purchased for noncommercial or home use. Occurs for 3 days annually during August.
- Solar access rights law prevents any community association from prohibiting a solar energy collection device on a property; however, associations may establish reasonable restrictions regarding size, placement of devices
- Solar easement law allows property owners to create binding solar easements for the purpose of protecting and maintaining proper access to sunlight. Easements must be in writing and include certain terms and conditions.
- Wind energy zoning ordinance applies to small wind energy systems installed to produce on-site electricity. Ordinance addresses height, setback, noise, liability insurance, and minimum parcel size.

INCENTIVES

- *VirginiaSAVES* Green Community Loan Program
- Washington Gas
- Appalachian Power (Electric)
- Charlottesville Gas
- Dominion Virginia Power
- Columbia Gas of Virginia
- Arlington Country, home energy rebates
- Fairfax County, Conservation Assistance Program

WASHINGTON

POLICY

- Fuel mix disclosure required by investor-owned, municipal, and cooperative utility companies.
- Net metering permitted. Law applies to systems up to 100 kilowatts in capacity that generate electricity using solar, wind, hydro, and other renewable forms of energy.
- Sales tax exemption is available on solar photovoltaic systems, solar thermal, biomass, and other qualified systems.
- Solar easement law permits parties to enter into solar contracts voluntarily for the purpose of ensuring adequate exposure of a solar energy system.

- Homeowners' associations are prohibited from restricting the installation of solar panels. Guidelines related to visibility and aesthetic aspects are permitted.
- Solar permits and setback requirements are based on system size and other features of a solar photovoltaic system. Land use requirements apply to single-family, multi-family and residential small lot zones.
- Washington State Housing Finance Commission offers the *Energy Spark Program* which gives special considerations to homebuyers purchasing an energy-efficient home.
- Wind energy zoning ordinance applies to small wind energy systems installed to produce on-site electricity. Ordinance addresses height, setback, noise, liability insurance, and minimum parcel size.

INCENTIVES

- Avista Utilities
- Benton PUD
- Callam County PUD
- Cascade Natural Gas
- Chelan County PUD
- Clark Public Utilities
- Columbia Rural Electric Association
- Cowlitz County PUD
- Franklin County PUD
- Grays Harbor PUD
- Inland Power & Light Company
- Lewis County PUD
- Mason County PUD
- Okanogan County PUD
- Orcas Power and Light
- Pacific Power
- Pend Oreille PUD
- Peninsula Light Company
- Port Angeles Public Works & Utilities
- Puget Sound Energy
- Richland Energy Services
- Seattle City Light
- Tacoma Power
- Vera Water & Power

WEST VIRGINIA

POLICY

- Net metering is available to all retail electricity customers using alternative or renewable sources of energy.
- Solar access rights law restricts housing associations from prohibiting solar energy system installation on homes. However, housing association members may vote to establish or remove a restriction.
- Wind energy zoning ordinance applies to small wind energy systems installed to produce on-site electricity. Ordinance addresses height, setback, noise, liability insurance, and minimum parcel size.

INCENTIVES

- Appalachian Power Company

WISCONSIN

POLICY

- Net metering is available to utility customers who generate excess electricity with systems up to 20 kilowatts in capacity. Law applies to investor-owned utilities, but not to electric cooperatives. Distributed-generation systems including renewable energy and combined heat and power systems are eligible.
- PACE financing approved and administered by local municipalities.
- Property tax exemption is available to homeowners who install renewable energy systems, including solar energy, wind, biogas, and other qualified systems.
- Sales tax exemptions apply to renewable energy, wood, biomass, and other qualifying sources.
- Solar and wind access rights law protects a resident's right to install and operate a solar or wind energy system. Law grants residents the right to have unrestricted access to the sun, and prohibiting neighbors from blocking sunlight. Homeowners' associations are prohibited from restricting solar energy systems.
- Wind energy zoning ordinance applies to small wind energy systems installed to produce on-site electricity. Ordinance addresses height, setback, noise, liability insurance, and minimum parcel size.

INCENTIVES

- Barron Electrical Cooperative
- Cedarburg Light and Water utility
- Eau Claire Energy Cooperative
- Home Performance Heating and Cooling program is eligible to residents and available from most utility companies and municipalities.
- Marshfield Utilities
- Milwaukee (City of)
- River Falls Municipal Utilities
- Riverland Energy Cooperative
- We Energies
- Xcel Energy

WYOMING

POLICY

- *Energy Savers* loans from Wyoming Community Development Authority are available to qualified homeowners for energy-efficient home retrofits. Income restrictions apply.
- Net metering available statewide; applies to investor-owned utilities, electric cooperatives, and irrigation districts. Eligible technologies include solar, wind, biomass, and hydropower systems up to 25 kilowatts.
- PACE financing is approved and administered by local municipalities.
- Solar Rights Act states that the beneficial use of solar energy is a property right, and landowner has right against interference with sunlight for the purpose of solar energy.
- Wind energy zoning ordinance applies to small wind energy systems installed to produce on-site electricity. Ordinance addresses height, setback, noise, liability insurance, and minimum parcel size.

INCENTIVES

- Black Hills Energy
- Lower Valley Energy
- Rocky Mountain Power
- Questar Gas

U.S. Resource

Database of State Incentives for Renewables and Efficiency (DSIRE)
Managed and funded by the North Carolina Clean Energy Technology Center Fund, a part of the N.C. State Engineering Foundation.
https://www.dsireusa.org

Canada Resource

Natural Resources Canada
Directory of Energy Efficiency and Alternative Energy Programs in Canada. Financial Incentives by Province.
www.nrcan.gc.ca/energy-efficiency/energy-efficiency-homes/financial-incentive-province/4947

About the Author

Winner of three national book awards, **Anna DeSimone** is a respected expert in the housing industry, and author of *Housing Finance 2020* and *Welcome to the Agrihood*. She was founder and CEO of Bankers Advisory, a mortgage compliance audit firm based in Lexington, Massachusetts, now part of Clifton Larson Allen, LLP.

Anna has written over 40 industry handbooks used by professionals throughout the United States. She was a featured entrepreneur by *Forbes Magazine* and *Bloomberg Markets*, named one of *Housing Wire's* Women of Influence, and received awards from *Acquisitions International* and *Wealth and Finance Magazine*.

She writes feature articles on the topic of housing, and provides expert commentary for news media, television, and radio.

View Anna's blog and news articles on her website:
www.annadesimone.net

Notes

[1] Joint Center for Housing Studies, Harvard University, *Healthy Home Remodeling: Consumer Trends and Contractor Preparedness.* January 2019.

[2] Ibid.

[3] U.S. Department of Energy, *Home R_X: The Health Benefits of Home Performance.*

[4] Ibid.

[5] International Energy Agency.

[6] Ibid.

[7] Yale University School of Environment, *Yale Climate Connections.*

[8] Energy Star, *Features and Benefits of Energy Star Certified Homes.*

[9] Center for Sustainable Systems, University of Michigan, *Residential Buildings Factsheet*, October 2020.

[10] U.S. Energy Information Administration (EIA), *2020 Energy Outlook.*

[11] Energy Star, *Breaking Down the Typical Utility Bill.*

[12] Center for Sustainable Systems, University of Michigan, *Residential Buildings Factsheet*, October 2020.

[13] Center for Sustainable Systems, University of Michigan, *Residential Buildings Factsheet,* October 2020.

[14] Natural Resources Canada, Heating Equipment for Residential Use.

[15] U.S. Department of Energy, Clean Energy.

[16] Center for Sustainable Systems, University of Michigan, *Greenhouse Gases Factsheet*, September 2020.

[17] Environmental Protection Agency, *Sources of Greenhouse Gas Emissions*.

[18] Center for Sustainable Systems, University of Michigan, *Carbon Footprint Factsheet*, September 2020.

[19] Environmental Protection Agency, *Household Carbon Footprint Calculator.*

[20] Ibid.

[21] United Nations Climate Change, *The Paris Agreement*.

[22] House of Commons of Canada, Bill C-12, An Act respecting transparency and accountability in Canada's efforts to achieve net zero greenhouse gas emissions by the year 2050.

[23] *Which Countries Have Legally Binding Net-Zero Emissions Targets*? James Murray, NS Energy, November 5, 2020.

[24] Energy Sage.

[25] Center for Sustainable Systems, University of Michigan, *Geothermal. Energy Factsheet,* September 2020.

[26] Canada Natural Resources, *Electricity Facts*

[27] Natural Resources Canada, Electricity Fact.

[28] Canada Wind Energy Association (CanWEA).

[29] U.S. Department of Energy.

[30] North Carolina Building Performance Association

[31] SEEFAR Building Analytics, Inc., *Monetizing Building Sustainability.*

[32] Building Science, Innovative Solutions for High-Performance Homes, *Durable Siding Options: Side by Side* by Juliet Grable.

[33] Ibid.

[34] James Hardie Building Products.

[35] Ibid.

[36] Green Builder, *Raise the Roof*, by Barbara Horwitz-Bennet.

[37] U.S. Department of Interior, Technical Preservation Services.

[38] Home Innovation Research Labs, *Insulation Use by Builders 2019.*

[39] U.S. Department of Energy, Insulation Materials.

[40] Energy Star, Environmental Protection Agency, Qualified Homes.

[41] Ibid.

[42] Ibid.

[43] U.S. Department of Energy, Heat Gain and Loss.

[44] Ibid.

[45] Ibid.

[46] Ibid.

[47] Energy Star.

[48] Energy Star, Environmental Protection Agency.

[49] Ibid.

[50] Ibid.

[51] U.S. Department of Energy, Heat and Cool, Home Heating Systems.

[52] Natural Resources Canada, Air Source Heat Pumps.

[53] U.S. Department of Energy, Heat and Cool, Heat Pump Systems.

[54] Ibid.

[55] Health Canada, *Choosing Between an HRV and an ERV,* Published by ECOHome, October 2020.
[56] Ibid.
[57] Ibid.
[58] U.S. Department of Energy, Moisture Control.
[59] Energy Star, Air Cooling, Fans.
[60] Environmental Protection Agency.
[61] Ibid.
[62] Energy Star, Environmental Protection Agency, Heating and Cooling.
[63] SEER Energy Savings.
[64] U.S. Department of Energy, *Heat and Cool, Evaporative Coolers.*
[65] Energy Star, *What is Energy Star.*
[66] Energy Star Canada, Natural Resources Canada.
[67] Ibid.
[68] Energy Star, *Lighting and Appliances.*
[69] Energy Star, *Lighting and Appliances.*
[70] U.S. Department of Energy, *Water Heating.*
[71] Environmental Protection Agency, *WaterSense.*
[72] Environmental Protection Agency, *Water Reuse and Recycling.*
[73] Energy Star, *Water Sense.*
[74] Environmental Protection Agency.
[75] Ibid.
[76] Environmental Protection Agency.
[77] Health Canada, *Guidelines for Canadian Drinking Water Quality.*
[78] Health Canada, *Be Well Aware.*
[79] U.S. Energy Information Administration, *Renewable Energy.*
[80] Ibid.
[81] Energy Rates Canada.
[82] Green Energy Efficient Homes.
[83] Center for Resource Solutions, *The Legal Basis for Renewable Energy Certificates*, 7/15/20.
[84] Energy Sage, SRECs: *Understanding Solar Renewable Energy Certificates.*
[85] Solar Reviews, *What is an SREC? Solar Renewable Energy Credits Explained,* December 31, 2020.
[86] SRECTrade, *Residential Market, Solar Credits Simplified.*

[87] Sol Systems, Residential SREC Selling Options.

[88] Environmental Protection Agency, *Solar Power Purchase Agreements.*

[89] NC Clean Energy Technology Center, *50 States of Solar.*

[90] E&E News, *U.S. suffers 147 Big Blackouts Each Year, October 2019.*

[91] Ibid.

[92] U.S. Department of Energy, *Energy Efficiency and Renewable Energy.*

[93] Energy Central, Power Industry Network, News Link, 12/9/2020.

[94] Energy Sage, *How Much Does a 10kW Solar System Cost?*

[95] Solar Reviews, *Why People Are Buying 10kw Solar, December 2020.*

[96] HES PV, Ltd., *Solar Energy*.

[97] Natural Resources Canada, *About Renewable Energy, Solar Energy*

[98] PV Magazine, *New Tool Calculates Solar Potential of Any Location in Canada, December 20, 2020.*

[99] Ibid.

[100] U.S. Department of Energy, Geothermal Energy.

[101] Center for Sustainable Systems, University of Michigan, *Geothermal Energy Factsheet,* September 2020.

[102] Energy Information Administration.

[103] Dandelion Energy.

[104] U.S. Department of Energy, Geothermal Energy.

[105] Natural Resources Canada, *Renewable Energy, Geothermal Energy.*

[106] Center for Sustainable Systems, University of Michigan, *Wind Energy Factsheet,* September 2020.

[107] U.S. Department of Energy, *Geothermal Energy.*

[108] U.S. Department of Energy, *Small and Community Wind.*

[109] Canada Wind Energy Association (CanWEA), *Wind Energy Vision,* April 2019.

[110] Natural Resources Canada, *Wind Energy.*

[111] Canadian Wind Energy Association (CanWEA).

[112] U.S. Department of Energy, *Microhydropower.*

[113] U.S. Department of Energy, *Bioenergy.*

[114] U.S. Department of Energy, *Four Cellulosic Ethanol Breakthroughs.*

[115] Natural Resources Canada.

[116] FP Innovations, *A Solid Wood Bioheat Guide for Rural and Remote Communities in Ontario.*

[117] Centre for Research and Innovation in the Bio-economy.

[118] Canada Home Builders' Association, Home Labelling Programs.

[119] World Green Building Council.

[120] Ibid.

[121] Zero Energy Project, *A Zero Carbon Building Primer*, Joe Emerson, April 2020.

[122] Eco Home, *Calculating the Carbon Footprint of Buildings, Introducing the EC3 Calculator from Skanska*, Bob Pierson, December 2019.

[123] Ibid.

[124] Zero Energy Project, *Positive Energy Homes, Solar Powered Vehicles.*

[125] Passive House Institute.

[126] Passive House Canada, *International Passive House Association. Brochure,* 2014.

[127] National Association of Home Builders, *Home Energy Labeling.*

[128] Canadian Home Builders Association, *Net Zero Home Labeling Program.*

[129] National Association of State Energy Officials.

[130] Environmental Protection Agency, *Energy Star Certified Homes.*

[131] Natural Resources Canada, *Energy Star Certified Homes.*

[132] National Green Building Standard, Innovative Research Labs.

[133] Natural Resources Canada*, R-2000.*

[134] U.S Department of Energy, *Zero Energy Ready Homes.*

[135] Energy Star, *Renewable Energy Ready Homes.*

[136] Canadian Home Builders' Association, *Net Zero Home Labeling Program.*

[137] Ibid.

[138] Zero Energy Project.

[139] Residential Energy Services Network, *HERS Energy Rating.*

[140] Ibid.

[141] Ibid.

[142] RESENT, *Water Efficiency Rating System.*

[143] Natural Resources Canada, *EnerGuide Energy Efficiency Home Evaluations.*

[144] U.S. Department of Energy, *Home Energy Score.*

[145] Business Wire, A Berkshire Hathaway Company, *Global Single-Family Modular and Prefabricated Housing Construction Market Report (2020-2023), August, 2020.*

[146] National Modular Housing Council.

[147] Canadian Home Builders' Association, Modular Construction Council.

[148] Metal Building Homes, *"Is There a Difference Between Modular and Prefab Homes?" May, 2020.*

[149] Manufactured Housing Institute, *2020 Manufactured Housing Facts.*

[150] Energy Star, *Energy Star Certified Manufactured Homes.*

[151] Artisan Log and Timber Homes, *The Carbon Footprint of a Log Home,* 2019.

[152] Ibid.

[153] Log and Timber Home Living Magazine.

[154] Environmental Protection Agency, *Mold.*

[155] Ibid.

[156] Environmental Protection Agency, *A Citizens Guide to Radon.*

[157] Ibid.

[158] Ibid.

[159] DMI AccuSystems, Old Saybrook, CT.

[160] Health Canada, *Radon.*

[161] Public Health Infobase of the Government of Canada, *Radon.*

[162] Environmental Protection Agency, *Carbon Monoxide.*

[163] Ibid.

[164] Health Canada, *Carbon Monoxide.*

[165] Environmental Protection Agency, *Nitrogen Dioxide.*

[166] Environmental Protection Agency, *Volatile Organic Chemicals.*

[167] Health Canada, *Volatile Organic Chemicals.*

[168] Environmental Protection Agency, *Volatile Organic Chemicals.*

[169] Health Canada, *Volatile Organic Chemicals.*

[170] Environmental Protection Agency, *Volatile Organic Chemicals.*

[171] U.S. Department of Housing and Urban Development, *Healthy House.*

[172] Ibid.

[173] Ibid.

[174] Health Canada, *Pesticide Safety.*

[175] Animal Wellness, *Protecting Your Pet from Indoor Air Pollution, November 2018.*

[176] Appraisal Institute, *Residential Green and Energy-Efficient Addendum.*

[177] Canada National Housing Strategy, *First Time Home Buyer Incentive.*

[178] Ibid.

[179] Freddie Mac, *GreenCHOICE Mortgage.*

[180] Freddie Mac, *Affordable Seconds.*

[181] Fannie Mae, *HomeStyle Energy.*

[182] Fannie Mae, *Community Seconds.*

[183] U.S. Dept. of Housing and Urban Development, *FHA Energy Efficient Mortgage Program.*

[184] FHA Solar and Wind Technologies.

[185] Canada Housing Mortgage Corporation, *Green Home Program.*

[186] Canada Guaranty *Energy-Efficient Advantage Program.*

[187] CoreLogic Home Price Index, October, 2020.

[188] Zillow, November 2020 article by Zillow, *Home Values Rising Faster than at Any Time Since 2005*, November 20, 2020.

[189] Global Property Guide, *Canada's Red Hot Housing Market*, by Lalaine C. Delmendo, January 28, 2021.

[190] Freddie Mac, Energy Efficiency: *Value Added to Properties and Loan Performance*, Robert Argento, Xian Fang Bank, and Lariece M. Brown.

[191] North Carolina Building Performance Association.

[192] North Carolina Energy Efficiency Alliance, *Energy Star Market Impact Study.*

[193] Rocky Mountain Institute, *The Economics of Zero-Energy Homes—Single-Family Insight.* Updated 2019.

[194] Efficiency Vermont, *Net Zero Feasibility Study*, prepared by Maclay Architects, January 30, 2015.

[195] Berkley National Laboratory, *Selling into the Sun: Price Premium Analysis of a Multi-State Dataset of Solar Homes*, January 13, 2015.

[196] Berkley National Laboratory Environmental Energy Technologies Division, *A Meta-Analysis of Single-Family Deep Energy Retrofit Performance in the U.S.,* Brennan Less and Iain Walker, 2014.

[197] SEEFAR Building Analytics, Inc.

[198] Ibid.

[199] Zillow, *Unexpected Repairs and Maintenance Tops the List of Regrets for Homeowners* by Kathryn Coursolle and Manny Garcia, May 29, 2019.

Index

Page Location of Primary Description

Books by Anna DeSimone

Housing Finance 2020

New Mortgage Programs for the New Generation of Homebuyers

Axiom Book Award Winner

Welcome to the Agrihood

Housing, Shopping, and Gardening for a Farm-to-Table Lifestyle

Pinnacle Book Achievement Award

Living Now Book Award

CPSIA information can be obtained
at www.ICGtesting.com
Printed in the USA
LVHW030547230322
714106LV00016B/2011

9 781039 123489